ALSO BY EVE LaPLANTE

Marmee & Louisa

Salem Witch Judge

American Jezebel

Seized

My Heart Is Boundless

Writings of
Abigail May Alcott,
Louisa's Mother

EDITED BY

Eve LaPlante

FREE PRESS

New York   London   Toronto   Sydney   New Delhi

FREE PRESS
A Division of Simon & Schuster, Inc.
1230 Avenue of the Americas
New York, NY 10020

First Free Press trade paperback edition November 2012

FREE PRESS and colophon are trademarks of Simon & Schuster, Inc.

For information about special discounts for bulk purchases,
please contact Simon & Schuster Special Sales at 1-866-506-1949
or business@simonandschuster.com.

The Simon & Schuster Speakers Bureau can bring authors to your live event.
For more information or to book an event contact the Simon & Schuster Speakers
Bureau at 1-866-248-3049 or visit our website at www.simonspeakers.com.

Manufactured in the United States of America

Permissions and credits for quotations in text are on pages 239–41

1   3   5   7   9   10   8   6   4   2

Library of Congress Cataloging-in-Publication Data

Alcott, Abigail May, 1800–1877.
My heart is boundless : writings of Abigail May Alcott, Louisa's mother /
edited by Eve LaPlante. — 1st Free Press trade paperback ed.
p. cm.
1. Alcott, Abba May, 1800-1877—Diaries. 2. Alcott, Abba May, 1800–1877—
Correspondence. 3. New England—Social life and customs—19th century.
4. Transcendentalists (New England)—Biography. 5. New England—Biography.
6. Alcott, Louisa May, 1832–1888—Family. I. LaPlante, Eve. II. Title.
CT275.A46A3 2012
974'.03092—dc23
[B]   2012034874

ISBN 978–1–4767–0280–3
ISBN 978–1–4767–0281–0 (ebook)

To Anna, Louisa, Elizabeth, and May,
and Rose, Clara, Charlotte, and Philip

My heart is as boundless as eternity. . . .

—Abigail May to her brother
Samuel Joseph, 1828

Contents

Introduction

Abigail May Alcott, the mother of Louisa, was the inspiration for one of the most beloved characters in American literature, *Little Women*'s Marmee. Born in Boston in 1800 and raised without formal schooling, Abigail struggled to educate herself, worked to support her family, encouraged her daughters' careers, and dedicated herself to ensuring equal rights for women and to ending slavery. A gifted writer, she composed hundreds if not thousands of letters and kept a journal from the time she was ten. But because her daughter and husband burned some of her letters and journals after her death, in 1877, scholars have long assumed that Abigail's papers no longer exist. "Where will you get your information about Abigail?" one of Louisa's biographers asked me a few years ago as I began work on *Marmee & Louisa,* a biography of the Alcott mother and daughter. "There's nothing there."

It is true that in her seventies Abigail asked Louisa to destroy all her private papers, hoping to protect her family and especially her husband from embarrassing revelations about their private lives and unhappy marriage. Louisa attempted after her mother's death to fulfill Abigail's wish but found she could not bear to complete the task any more than she could burn all of her own letters and journals, as Louisa told at least one friend she wished to do. Meanwhile, Abigail's widower, Bronson Alcott, edited, rewrote, and did burn some of his late wife's papers. No one will ever know the contents of what he destroyed. But we can infer that it contained information even more intimate and troubling than what survives about his failure to support his family and his apparent indifference to their physical and emotional needs. Collections of Alcott papers contain numerous references to the alteration of family documents. "53 Destroyed. Letters 1861," a curator wrote in a volume of Abigail's original letters at Harvard's Houghton Library from which scores of pages were obviously cut out. Inside the volume's cover a descendant wrote, "Some letters have been destroyed by family, as unnecessary and unsuitable for others' inspection, reflecting hardship & troubles of personal nature. Many letters herein have been copied & are so marked in red pencil by A.B. Alcott, for use in the life of his wife he had planned to publish." The bound volumes that Bronson kept of his own letters are littered with curators' notations such as "numerous excisions . . . some excisions . . . numerous excisions."

And yet, despite all the Alcotts' efforts to purge the family record, thousands of Abigail's words, in hundreds of pages of letters and journals, remain in archival and private collections, mostly unpublished and unexamined. In exploring these collections while preparing this volume, I have been amazed at the amount of material that still exists in Abigail's hand. It is an unexpected trove and, as I discovered while writing *Marmee & Louisa,* a biographer's dream.

My Heart Is Boundless, the first compilation of Abigail's writings, is a sampling of her extant papers, meant to convey the spirit rather than the whole. Future investigations will no doubt unearth more of Abigail's private papers, just as works of her famous daughter continue to be discovered in attic trunks. Two letters from Abigail to a friend were discovered in the early twenty-first century in the house in western Maine to which she had mailed them in 1848. *My Heart Is Boundless* includes her letters, journal entries, and other miscellaneous papers, including a few recipes. Most of these documents are in the collections of Harvard University and Orchard House, the Alcott museum and educational center in Concord, Massachusetts. I also include portions of previously unknown family letters describing May and Alcott family life from the 1830s to the 1870s. Among the many subjects that possessed Abigail are mother-daughter relationships, childrearing, marriage and divorce, success, education, slavery and abolition, female suffrage, diet, health, cooking, housekeeping, male-female relationships, and death. In this collection I have arranged her papers chronologically by subject, so that an entry Abigail wrote during her sixties about her childhood appears in the childhood section. All available information about the date and place of composition is included in the text or explanatory notes.

Abigail encouraged Louisa to write and in many senses gave Louisa her voice. On the page Abigail herself comes across as theatrical, poignant, passionate, and often satirical. She seemed effortlessly to coin aphorisms, such as:

> *In this world of folly and fashion,*
> *a man's hat is the most essential part of his head.*

> *Wisdom must be fed and clothed,*
> *and neither the butcher nor tailor*
> *will take pay in aphorisms or hypotheses.*

> *We are all part and parcel of this condition of things,*
> *and I for one am a restless fragment and can't find my niche.*

> *Some flowers give out little or no odour, until crushed.*

Indeed, some scholars consider Abigail "a better writer than her more famous daughter," according to the Alcott family biographer Madelon Bedell. That is for the reader to decide. Ironically, Abigail's celebrated husband, though a charismatic speaker, could not write a lucid sentence to save his life, according to many who knew him. As James Russell Lowell wrote of Bronson, "While he talks he is great but goes out like a taper / If you shut him up closely with pen, ink, and paper." Abigail, on the other hand, was fully herself with pen, ink, and paper, as I hope this collection will demonstrate.

One aim of *My Heart Is Boundless* is to answer the fundamental question, Who was Abigail May Alcott? To her four children she was "Marmee." To her husband she was a skilled housewife, excelling at domestic pursuits. To her daughter she was the person to whom Louisa felt closest in the world. Abigail gave Louisa her first journal, pushed her to write, and served as her mentor and muse. Louisa in turn pored over her mother's journals and private papers in writing her novels and stories, at Abigail's own insistence, and based many of those tales on Abigail's character and experiences. Abigail's actual words, many of them published here for the first time, illuminate the inner life of a remarkable nineteenth-century woman. I hope that *My Heart Is Boundless* will show Abigail May Alcott to be not just a mother, housewife, or even mentor to Louisa, but also an American writer and thinker who has too long been ignored.

—Eve LaPlante, August 2012

My Heart Is Boundless

Early Years

*N*ear the end of her life, in 1872, and prompted in part by her family's *newfound celebrity in the wake of* Little Women, *Abigail composed an autobiographical sketch. Six years later, not long after her death, Bronson used this sketch as the basis of a manuscript he hoped to publish as his wife's "Memoir of 1878." There is no evidence of its publication, but small portions of the sketch will provide context throughout* My Heart Is Boundless.

Abigail's Autobiographical Sketch

I wish to record here as briefly as possible some of the events of my early life. I was born in Boston, October 8, 1800. My name was given me for my grandmother, Abigail Williams. I was christened at the Stone Chapel by Rev. R. James Freeman.★ My father was Joseph May, my mother Dorothy Sewall. I was the youngest of twelve children, born sickly, nursed by a sickly woman, and at six months was badly burned on the face and right hand.†

My mother was Dorothy Sewall, daughter of Samuel Sewall of Boston, by his wife Elizabeth Quincy, niece of Josiah Quincy of Revolutionary memory, and sister of Dorothy, the wife of John

---

★"Stone Chapel" was the name patriots used for King's Chapel to avoid mentioning the monarchy. King's Chapel still stands in downtown Boston, at the corner of Tremont and School streets.

†Of the twelve May children, only three—Charles, Samuel Joseph, and Abigail—survived to middle age.

Hancock, for whom my mother was named. Though her own education had been a limited one, [my mother] was constantly solicitous that her daughters should be educated as fit companions for man. My [maternal] great-grandfather was Rev. Joseph Sewall of the Third Church.★ My direct ancestor, the father of Rev. Dr. Sewall, was Chief Justice [Samuel] Sewall (born in England 1652, died in Boston 1730).†

My father, Joseph May, was born March 25, 1760. His father, Samuel May, lived at that time at the South End of Boston, between what is now called Decatur Street and Davis Street. The town pier stood directly in front of his house. [My grandfather] kept a lumber wharf, the wake flowing on to his back yard, which extended to what is now called Harrison Street. My father . . . led a useful honorable life . . . and was never known to do a mean or selfish act. . . . He was truly a father of the fatherless and the widow's friend. My father read a good deal when his office duties were over, and he was fond of furnishing me with good reading. He had a fine library, many rare books. He was for many years commander of the Cadets [of the Ancient and Honorable Artillery] and for forty years warden of King's Chapel. He died February 27, 1841.

This antique little document was given me by my Father in 1840:

"Boston, 28 May 1801, Received of Joseph May Sixty-two dollars, in full for nursing his daughter Abigail, thirty-one weeks from 9th of October last . . . in full amount. Ebenezer Leland."‡

Owing to my delicate health I was much indulged [as a child],

---

★The Rev. Joseph Sewall (1688–1762) was minister of Boston's Third Church for much of the eighteenth century. That church, now known as the Old South Meeting House, is a historic site open to the public, on Washington Street.

†Judge Samuel Sewall (1652–1730) was the only Salem witch judge who repented for having executed innocent people as witches in 1692. He was the author of America's first antislavery tract, *The Selling of Joseph* (1700), and an early argument for equal rights for women, *Talitha Cumi* (1725).

‡This appears to be a doctor's bill for Abigail's birth, paid in installments.

allowed to read a great deal, fed on nice food, and had many indulgences not given my sisters and brothers. I was rather a good child, but willful. My schooling was much interrupted by ill health. I read aloud a good deal to my mother and sisters when they were employed. I never cared much for society; parties I disliked. I danced well and remember at Mr. Turner's school (1812–14) having for partners some boys who afterward became eminent divines.*

Miss Eliza Robbins was my teacher three years, from 1813 to 1816. She had a remarkable faculty for illustrating her lessons. There was no drone or loafer near her. She made each girl use the talents she had, to the best advantage. I can add my tribute of respect to her talents and excellence, and I shall cherish a grateful remembrance for all she was to me at that important period of my life. She was author of *Popular Sermons, Poetry for Children,* and other excellent schoolbooks. She died in July 1853.

Abigail's father, who worked in business and insurance, sought the best education possible for his sons, and expected his four daughters to marry well and succeed as wives and mothers. Abigail's "willfulness" worried him, as he suggested to her in a letter when she was ten.

To Abigail from her father

Boston, September 6, 1811

Dear Abby,

"To be good is to be happy" is an old maxim, one to which I pay great respect and can recommend it to my young friends, who are inexperienced in the ways of the world. Attention, kindness, gentleness, good nature, and a desire to please, tend to procure friends, and to diffuse pleasure to all around us; while industry, patience,

---

*Divines are ministers.

perseverance, fidelity, and a desire to excel, make us useful and
valuable members of society; and moral virtue, piety, and resignation, secure us peace in our bosoms, and the Smile of our heavenly
Father. This [illegible] I hope will make a strong impression on
your mind. You have lived much at home, and are now old enough
to begin to see and know how other folk live, and how they conduct
[themselves].

*In spite of her father's conventional goals, Abigail thirsted for the education
that was afforded her brother by virtue of gender. While the four May sisters
were tutored part-time at home after attending a few years of Ma'am school,★
her brother Samuel Joseph was prepared for college at the exclusive Chauncy
Hall School, enrolled at Harvard College at fifteen, and graduated from Harvard Divinity School. Watching him, Abigail yearned to read history and
literature, to learn Latin and Greek, and to use her mind to improve the
world, as he was encouraged to do. Neither her father nor her society valued
these goals in a girl, but Samuel Joseph, three years her senior, honored her
ambition and devoted himself to aiding her in educating herself.*

To Abigail, fourteen, from her
seventeen-year-old brother at Harvard

Cambridge, August 14, 1815

My dear sister,

I assured you in my call and perhaps convinced you that there
are no such things as innate ideas, at least you must take it for
granted unless you prove the contrary, for if there were innate ideas
all Mr. [John] Locke's endeavors to prove how we acquired our

---

★Ma'am, or dame, schools were female-run, at-home schools for young
children.

knowledge would be useless, and it would be lost labor in me to try to show you what I have insisted to in my letters on Mr. Locke's theory reflecting the origins of our ideas. I am so often interrupted and have so many calls upon my time that I shall not be able in this letter to finish with this topic, as I could wish. I should therefore leave the consideration of it till my next. I received your letter just as I gave mine to the stage driver or I should have acknowledged the arrival of it. Your conception of the meaning which Mr. Locke intends to convey, when he denies that there are any innate ideas, is I believe, similar to that of most people, and I do not deny that it is a reasonable inference from the general tenor of his discourse, though I believe he in no place makes a direct assertion to that affect.

What you say relative to education is certainly true. Nothing is of unimportance in the formation of the mind. (But more of education later.) You ask, "Why a man born blind can tell the color of a thing by touch?" I did not know that was the case, but I think I can show you how it would be possible. You know it is said and I believe proved that where a person is deprived of the use of one faculty, the others are proportionately augmented. Therefore when a piece of red or yellow silk is applied to the touch of a blind man, that sense in him is so strong that he is able through it to perceive something peculiar to that silk which he ever after retains in his mind, or in other words has an idea of yellow silk, though he cannot have one of colors. . . .

But more when we meet, S. J. May

All of Abigail's sisters followed a young woman's expected path by marrying suitable men and bearing children. Her sister Eliza was only seventeen at her wedding, in 1817. Not long before that wedding, Abigail, sixteen, and Eliza were visiting the family of Eliza's intended, Benjamin Willis, in Portland, Maine.

From Abigail to her parents

Portland [Maine], Saturday, April 26, 1817

Well, my dear Parents, your girls have not set off yet. Our dear friends were so urgent for our stay that we could not with propriety leave them. We shall, however, leave here next week. We engaged our passage on board the *Messenger,* but before we were summoned we received your letter. Uncle sent a word to Capt Lowell that the Miss Mays would not go till next week. All we could say was to no avail. He would be obeyed. We had a charming letter from brother Sam. . . . When did you hear from [my] dear [sister] Louisa? We both wrote her a long letter on Saturday. I hope to meet the dear girl 'ere long. And soon I hope we shall all meet our dear parents in health.

Dear Parents, we shall return soon, and then, I promise you, will make the house laugh. Good bye and goodby, soon may you kiss your affectionate daughter, Abby.

From Abigail, seventeen, to her father

Portland, May 4, 1818

To Col. May,

Indeed, dear father, we have been strangers, no communication whatever. I told Louisa I was half a mind to be affronted with you because you were so silent.★ However your kind, delightful letter made all up, so [we] will kiss and be friends.

I am afraid I am too hard with my correspondents. I require too much of them. I love to write letters (when I may be allowed to talk my own language) to my dear friends, and I love still more to receive them. . . .

★The Louisa referred to here is Abigail's sister, eleven years older.

I wish I was near, just to comb your head a bit and get a kiss, before I say goodnight. But I must tell you I am Abby, your affectionate daughter, and be off.

Autobiographical sketch

In 1819 I went by the advice of my brother Samuel J. May to pass a year with his friend Miss Allyn of Duxbury, who assisted me in reviewing my studies.* She became a most valuable teacher and aid in every way. With her I studied French, Latin, and Botany,† and read History, very extensively, making notes of many works, such as Hume, Gibbon's *Rise and Fall of the Roman Empire,* Hallam's *Middle Ages,* Robertson's *Charles 5th,* Goldsmith, Rollin, and many others.‡ I did not love study, but books were always attractive.

From Abigail, eighteen, to her parents

Duxbury [Massachusetts], March 25, 1819
I cannot but think a further knowledge of myself and my situation will please you, my dear parents, and with this impulse, joined with that of ability to do it, I write you with pleasure. . . . My mind, char-

---

*Abby Allyn and her brother the Rev. John Allyn housed and provided instruction to eighteen-year-old Abigail that year.

†With the Allyns Abigail also studied geometry, astronomy, chemistry, moral philosophy (with an emphasis on the Scottish Enlightenment), and natural theology.

‡The books mentioned are David Hume's *History of England,* Edward Gibbon's *Decline and Fall of the Roman Empire,* Henry Hallam's *View of the State of Europe During the Middle Ages,* William Robertson's *History of Charles 5th,* Oliver Goldsmith's four-volume *History of England,* and Charles Rollin's *Ancient History of the Egyptians, Carthaginians, Assyrians, Babylonians, Medes and Persians, Macedonians and Grecians.*

acter, and feelings are more under the control of reason than they have been. Under the constant direction of Miss Allyn my mind is cultivated and improved. She thinks the soil is not bad. This gives me assurance and excites me to action. I have nothing here to excite *bad* feelings, therefore by constantly entertaining good ones, I am in hopes they will become habitual, and strengthen with my strength.

Miss Allyn is a model worthy of imitation. By her character I form my own, and the very impossibility of being like her incites me to constant attention. From Louisa's and Sam's letters you probably have learned my subjects and studies, but I advance daily, and therefore my studies change or rather the course of reading varies them. We are at present . . . reading Stewart's Essays, Miss Adams's *History of New England,* and Bonnycastle's *Astronomy* in the evening. In the morning I get a lesson in *Historia Sacra* and Grammar and read till dinner time in Miss Adams's *History*. In the afternoon, two hours in Latin, two in Chemistry. In the evening [I read] in Bonnycastle with the globe and heaven to help me in comprehending this wonderful and sublime science. The heaven declares the Glory of God. The wisest and greatest men, both ancient and modern, confess themselves charmed with it. I can wish with Virgil who spoke of it with enthusiasm.

On Sunday we read Paley's *Horae Paulinae* with the Epistles in the Bible. We have finished his *Evidence*s, which have enlarged my ideas of Christianity wonderfully. Hutchinson's *History of Massachusetts* with Holmes's *Annals* and Belknap's *Lives* have given me a thorough knowledge of our country. But Miss Allyn thought Miss Adams's *History* good, and gave me that. . . . I have finished Ramsey's *Life of Washington,* with an account of the American Revolution. This has interested me so much.

As regards the study of Latin, I do not know what your opinion is, but I should like it. . . . The Dr. and Miss Allyn advised it warmly.★

★"The Doctor" is the Rev. John Allyn, Miss Allyn's brother.

The Doctor thought it would give me a more perfect knowledge of my own language, and enable me to detect errors which otherwise would pass unnoticed. Miss Allyn thought it an exercise for the mind, memory, and attention. And as it does not prevent my pursuing other things of more importance, I have undertaken it, and have got as far as Cain and Abel in my *Historia Sacra* to parse. I continue a chapter in John, in the Latin testament, every Sunday, and

> *I am not willing to be thought incapable of any thing.*

am elated with my progress. I wrote to my brother to say nothing of this, for if I should not succeed I should be mortified to have you know it. I wish my pride was subdued as regards this. I am not willing to be thought incapable of any thing.

I have received a long letter from my brother. This good fellow has done so much for me that I cannot thank him, and am obliged to be silent and show my gratitude by improvement. He has written me often, and it does me much good to have letters from home. I wish you both would write me. . . .

The Dr. [Allyn] desires [I send you] his regards, thinks he knows you very well, and often describes your person and character—the red gaiters, mixed stockings, little bow in your cravat, and a thousand beauties which a partial daughter loves to talk about and describe. Miss Allyn says she was a neighbor of yours when you lived in Cross St. You assisted them at the death of her father. She and her sister were alone, and she says you kindly reproved them for not sending for you before, and with tears in her eyes says you are the best man that ever lived. And my mother sent them in some salmon for dinner the day before the funeral. . . .

I came here a stranger, and now I am provided with friends. This is delightfully flattering. I hope it is because I am good. I wish it was a possible thing to get a Caesar for Miss Allyn . . . do gratify me by buying it. . . . Miss Allyn has come to read [with me], and I must not break in upon our rule, for she does not herself. She puts every thing aside for order, and order is your first law. Remember I love you dearly; apprise me of your affection by an early letter to

Your affectionate daughter

To her sister Eliza May Willis, married with a newborn son

Duxbury, July 1819

Dear Eliza,

. . . You have been in my mind for these four days, almost sole proprietor, and sometimes intruder. I have made it a point of confidence not to think of home and home friends when I can be gaining a single new idea. . . .

A long letter from Louisa has awakened a remembrance of the delightful visit I spent in Portland a year this season and to strengthening all my resolutions. I must think of my sisters and their appendages.* The sweet boy comes next in my mind's eye. . . . I wish I could share your enjoyment in watching his advancement. Soon he will be whispering in your ear what hitherto he has only been able to show by fondness and winning looks, that he dearly loves you; soon he will be rivaling his Aunt [Abigail] in *amo, amas, amat,* . . . And may he like her thirst for knowledge, but, unlike her, may he be earlier gratified and better able to receive the draught, which intoxicates weak minds, but renders strong minds stronger. I could fill my paper with reflections on the sweet fellow, my hopes, wishes, expectation in his behalf, but the mother must be remembered, and to her I have a thousand things to say. . . .

Eliza, though a wife, though a mother, you are still a daughter and a sister, and permit me [to] share your pleasure and pains. I once was

---

*"Appendages" refers to her sisters' children.

your twin sister.* I trust in a great measure I am so now. But I feel a separation, a division, a something which I cannot describe. I seem gradually to be losing my knowledge of yourself, your character, mind, person, . . . and I fear, I dread an indifference may ensue. . . .

Your pursuits in life will probably be very different from mine, but still we may sympathize in feelings if not in action. . . . I may yet earn my bread by the knowledge this year has afforded me and spend the medium of [my] life in teaching a school. . . . I am strain-

> *I am straining every nerve of my mind and heart to be what I should be.*

ing every nerve of my mind and heart to be what I should be. . . .

You see, my dear girl, how fulfilled I have been; my letter abounds in *Ego*. . . .

Your affectionate Sister A.

Before agreeing to return from Duxbury to her parents' house in Boston, Abigail exacted from them a promise that they permit her to avoid socializing with young men, in order to continue her studies. Her father had encouraged her to accept a marriage proposal from his nephew, twenty-nine-year-old Samuel May Frothingham, of Portland, Maine. Abigail liked her cousin but was not sure she wished to be married. She desired an education and then, she hoped, to write or teach, two of the few professions open to single women.[†]

To her parents

Duxbury, October 8–10, 1819

Dear Father and Mother,

About returning home after an absence of ten months . . . [and]

---

*Abigail and Eliza May were only a year apart in age.

†Other professions open to single women were housekeeping, sewing, and other domestic arts. Married women of Abigail's social class did not work outside the home.

concluding the happiest term of my past life . . . I am naturally led to the retrospect, and am constantly reflecting on plans for my future good. This I often do, alone by myself, calmly. To my father and mother I would make known the result of my retrospective views, and consult on plans for my future good.

This day makes me nineteen years of age. Many of these years have been passed in trifling occupations, or wanton negligence, "talents wasted, time misspent." But I have already consumed hours in unprofitable regrets. . . . Ten months have made me a new being within myself. . . .

I am resolved and nothing shall move me. I should like this winter to devote *much* of my time in study. . . . I am willing to do my share in the family, and more than my share, if I may be allowed to refuse visiting. This has been for a year or two one of the greatest taxes on me; and I *must* be permitted this winter to withdraw, or rather not to enter again those gay scenes where once was my delight. For visiting is altogether incompatible with study, and improvement. I own that some good may be gained in some circles, but in selecting friends, you give offense: it is better to treat everybody well, and be intimate with nobody. I cannot let this winter pass without much improvement in mind and habits. I feel as if I had just begun life, for I never enjoyed life rationally before. And I am every day more convinced that there are no real enjoyments but those which philosophy dictates and religion sanctions. . . .

You see, dear Parents, I am making *Ego* the heroine of my narrative. But Ego to me has been for several months the most interesting character I ever knew. . . . I have completed nothing, but I have begun much. I have nothing to show, but I have much to *do*. An education can never be completed; we must constantly progress in knowledge and virtue, or we must deteriorate. . . .

People often fear public opinion. . . . It shall be different with me. If I incur the epithet pedantic, or unsocial, or misanthropic, I must bear it patiently, and by the approbation of my own conscience, and those near friends who know my motives for excluding myself a little while from a gay circle, must outlive the unjust epithets bestowed upon me, and trust that time will obliterate the fiction of opinion, and confirm the decisions of truth.

I shall return in a fortnight. I wish you could come for me. The Dr and Miss Allyn would be highly gratified; it would be a delightful chance to take me home, and the ride would do you good. Let me have another of your kind letters. . . .

> Your affectionate and grateful daughter, A.

Autobiographical sketch

August 2, 1819, I was called home [from Miss Allyn's school] by the death of a dear cousin, Samuel M[ay] Frothingham, to whom I had virtually betrothed my affections.

My oldest sister, Catherine May Windship, died at Roxbury, Massachusetts on March 14, 1815. Her widower was Charles Williams Windship, E.D.

Elizabeth [Eliza] Sewall May married Benjamin Willis and died at Portland [Maine], March 4, 1822.

Mr. [Samuel] Greele married Miss Louisa May, October 17, 1823.

By the time Abigail was twenty-three, all her sisters—Catherine, Louisa, and Eliza—had gotten married and had children, and Catherine and Eliza had died. Abigail dreamed not of marriage but of opening a school at home or of writing. Meanwhile, Abigail had to spend much time in her twenties caring for her orphaned niece and nephews, Elizabeth Willis, Hamilton Willis, and Charles Windship. Abigail's sixty-six-year-old mother, who had been frail as long as Abigail could remember, died in October 1825. A few months earlier, Samuel Joseph had married Lucretia Flagge Coffin, who would become Abigail's closest female friend. In the late 1820s Abigail often brought her orphaned charges with her to stay with Samuel Joseph and Lucretia in Brooklyn, Connecticut, where he worked as a Unitarian minister. By 1828, with the death of their last surviving sister, Louisa May Greele, Abigail and Samuel Joseph were the only May siblings alive except a much older brother, Charles, who was absent during Abigail's early life.

To her father

July 1824, Brooklyn, Connecticut

Dear Father . . . In the afternoon I set out for Canterbury on Mr. Prince's nag.* I got about two rods from the house when the saddle slipped. I disengaged my foot in just time enough to jump clear from the horse. I remounted after convincing myself that I was light, and rode through the village in style to Mr. Bacchus's where my brother was taking tea. . . . I have often thought that an accident on horseback would lessen my courage, but these [accidents] have increased it. . . .

June 15, 1825, Brooklyn

. . . I am as happy as I ever expect to be in this life when I am with him [Samuel Joseph] and in Brooklyn, but I would not stay another moment if I thought I could give my mother sympathy. I am happy to be allowed the privilege of being with my dear Lucretia at this commencement, as it were, of her [married] life, and though our roads through life are wide apart, yet our horizon is the same. . . .

---

*Canterbury is a few miles south of Brooklyn, Connecticut.

Brooklyn, November 1825

... The dying countenance of my beloved mother is vivid in my mind, but not more so than the appropriateness of her life and the active benevolence that characterized it. Her life was one of toil, but her happy death was that of the slumbering Christian.

... I find that on Sunday my mind dwells on the memorable Sabbath that I passed in the chamber of my dying mother. The contemplation of her death rather tranquillizes than excites me. She has been constantly before me since I came here. . . .

Abby

Autobiographical sketch

My mother [Dorothy Sewall] lost her parents at the early age of nine years. An orphan, she went to reside with her grandfather Dr. [Joseph] Sewall of the Old South Church Boston. Her oldest sister, Elizabeth Sewall, married Mr. Samuel Salisbury, who took Dorothy, my mother, home with her to Worcester. In this family she became acquainted with my father, who was an apprentice in Mr. Salisbury's store. . . . After an engagement of nine years she married, being 24 years of age. . . . My mother's most striking trait was her affectionate disposition. She adored her husband and children. She loved the whole human family, and went about doing good. . . . Though her own education had been a limited one, she was constantly solicitous that her daughters should be educated as fit companions for man.

Not long after Dorothy Sewall May's death, Abigail's sixty-five-year-old father began courting the widow of a former assistant minister at their church. To Abigail's dismay, Colonel May was soon engaged to be married.

To a paternal cousin, Thomas May, of Richmond, Virginia

Boston, October 9, 1826

Dear Cousin,

My father has told me that he has not acknowledged the receipt of your acceptable offering. I reprimanded him severely, and he dared me to do it for him. . . .

My father has been very busy in conjugating the verb *to love,* and I assure you declines its *moods* and *tenses* inimitably. This is the only apology I can offer. . . .

To her father

Brooklyn [Connecticut], August 1, 1827

Dear Father,

I have lifted my foot from the rocker, seated my self at the minister's desk, for the purpose of thanking you for the expression of a wish that I should write you. . . .★ [Mr. Dewey] preached on Sunday admirably. I only heard one sermon. That was as much as I could contain and I fear more than I could digest. I am of the opinion that great moral impressions cannot be made in one day, and if I can hear one on the Sabbath, I am satisfied that the rest of the day may be spent in reflection and appropriate duties. . . . Help [from servants] is not to be had for love or money. The farmers' daughters prefer factories or trades; and those who from necessity live at service, work in the kitchen, but recreate in the parlor. This we could not endure: it engenders more mischief than is safe to be ventured.

★"The minister" is her brother Samuel Joseph.

Courtship and Marriage

*A*bigail May met Bronson Alcott in 1827 while staying with her brother's family in Brooklyn, Connecticut. Their courtship lasted nearly three years, during which they communicated mostly by letter. In the early spring of 1828, at the urging of Abigail's brother, Bronson moved to Boston, where he was hired to start an infant school, the equivalent of a modern preschool. Not long afterward, to be near Bronson, twenty-seven-year-old Abigail returned from Connecticut to live in her father and stepmother's house.

Autobiographical sketch

While at Brooklyn I met Mr. 'A. Bronson Alcott,' a teacher, professional Educator. His views on Education were very attractive to my brother as well as myself. I was charmed by his modesty, his earnest desire to promote better advantages for the young. Not an educated man himself, he was determined that the large fund of 1,000,000 (one million [dollars]) then given by Conn[ecticut] for educational purposes should be used for higher ends than they were appropriated to at that time. He concerted with Mr. May and they raised the salaries of the Common School Teachers and thus secured better teaching about this time.*

---

*"Mr. May" is her brother.

To Bronson Alcott

Brooklyn [Connecticut] Sept. 16, 1827

To Mr. Alcott,

Thank you, good Sire, for the kind remembrance you have manifested for Brooklyn friends. . . . Our infant is beautiful. . . .★ He laughs audibly at my facetious young "Little Bo Peep . . ."

This leads me to an interesting part of our conversation, Female Education, its defects and deficiencies, which have from time immemorial kept us in a latitude unrecognized and oppressive to our moral health and intellectual growth. The good [William] Russell has come forth as a pioneer to our emancipation.† He is gently removing the veil, and men are beginning to see that we are intelligent, accountable beings. He is continuously admitting the light of truth, having been taught by experience that truth is no welcome guest when it comes in the garb of innovation; and that ignorance is easily dazzled to blindness by the sudden light of knowledge. He has said that "Woman was the mother of man." Let us thank him for this, for it is a fact that has well nigh been forgotten.

That we are instruments in the hand of the Great Artificer cannot be denied.‡ Let us then be used as such. Let our women be treated as divine agents, not merely as objects of pleasure or sense created only for convenience and admiration. Let us be taught to think, to act, to teach; let us adopt and exercise the laws of our nature, which nature is Love. Newton's mother gave birth to her son three months after her husband's death. She early began to elevate her infant's mind to nature and nature's laws, allowing him to pursue

---

★"Our infant" is Samuel Joseph and Lucretia's first child, three-month-old Joseph.

†William Russell was a Scottish educational innovator who later started a school in Philadelphia with Bronson.

‡"Great Artificer" is God.

the bent of his inclination, taking care however that it should be an enlightened inclination. . . . Subject to such truth, should not woman be educated, enlightened?

. . . Should you go to Boston, as Mr. Russell intimates, in the spring, and should require a female assistant, and will in the interim consider me your pupil, instructing me in reference to this object, I should be pleased to associate myself with you for that purpose. At all counts, your instruction should not be lost, for there is a little circle who call me "Aunt" and I may serve them more effectually for having enjoyed your assistance. It would add much to my happiness to form an arc in your social circle wherever you may be. My words come dripping off my pen so fast that their component parts are lost. You will I fear be puzzled to read and more puzzled to understand; but the fear that my thoughts will be chilled by too much attention to their expression, has made my language incoherent, my writing shameful. But if amidst the scrawl, you can make out what I most wish to convey, I shall be satisfied, hoping that it will not discourage your benevolent intention of gratifying me by your letters. I shall pass the winter here and hope to hear from you (if not see you) often.

Wishing you success in all your undertakings, let me continue to pray that God, my refuge, may be your guide.

Respectfully, A.M.

To Samuel Joseph

Boston, May 1828

My dear brother, we are here, alive and well. Hope you get on to your heart's content, wifeless, childless, sisterless.* Noiseless. I

---

*Abigail, Lucretia, and little Joseph May were visiting at the May house in Boston, leaving Samuel Joseph alone in Connecticut.

can as yet tell you no news . . . [but] Louisa tells me Mr. Alcott is all the 'rage.' The Cabots are head over heels enamored with his system. . . . Susan Cabot says, "The Infant [school] may make us much [advantage] as they have a mind to if Mr. A[lcott] will only take the school." . . . Louisa has only seen him once. He is constantly with some of the grandees. . . . I have not seen him, do write to him. . . .

Again Abigail offered Bronson her services as an assistant teacher. Having already lost several teaching positions because parents objected to his unorthodox classroom style, and fearing she might remain as a teacher at the school after his anticipated departure, Bronson refused to work with her. Two months later, in August 1828, she boldly proposed marriage to him. Unable to speak, he handed her his journal, in which he had written of his admiration for her and her family.

To Bronson Alcott on their engagement

August [2,] 1828

Dear Mr. Alcott,

The thoughts of your journal handed me this evening are so in accordance with my own that I cannot quench the Spirit you have lighted up. . . . Why, my dear friend, is not physiology made a part of our education? Why should we not understand what we see, feel, suffer, enjoy? . . . We study mind, metaphysics, that we may the better regulate our own, and influence that of others.

None but the most depraved could derive any thing from it but what is beautiful, every thing to wonder and adore. Those who can pursue it from less pure motives can be compared only to the fiend who entered the Garden of Eden. Many of my sisters blush at that which if investigated would make them love God more profusely. . . . I may almost

I will never quench the ardor of my imagination.

say the object for which woman was created is forgotten or shunned as being unfit [for] their delicate sensibility to investigate. But where am I in a world of design. I will never quench the ardor of my imagination. But I will direct it to those channels where it shall gather flowers for the fancy, and food for the mind. . . .

To her brother Samuel Joseph, announcing her engagement

Boston, August 1828

My dear brother,

I should have answered your kind letter before, but ever since I wrote you last, my mind and heart have been on the stretch. I am engaged to Mr. Alcott not in a school, but in the solemn, the momentous capacity of friend and wife. He has been attached to me from the evening of your conversation in Brooklyn, but circumstances have prevented the disclosure of his feelings.* I found it remained for me to dissolve all connexion with him or give him that encouragement and promise which should secure to him my future interest. The former I could not do. I found myself clinging to his interests, distressed at his long absences. I found on analyzing my regard for him that I loved him and I therefore resolved on the latter condition.

I do think him in every respect qualified to make me happy. He is moderate, I am impetuous. He is prudent and humble, I am forward and arbitrary. He is poor, but we are both industrious. Why may we not be happy? He has made an exposition of his character to me, so simple, so pure, so just which Jesus loved. We talk little of heaven, but are already busy in schemes for our future independence and comfort.

---

*Samuel Joseph and Bronson's first conversation occurred in July 1827.

No being but Louisa Greele and Greenwood and Mother know this decision.★ I wish to have it kept profound untill [sic] I come back from Hingham, and by that time Mr A[lcott] will be fixed in his own school. I am afraid he is embarrassed a little in his circumstances. I did think the ladies ought to remunerate him generously.

Is there not some indirect way that you could manage it for him? Do write to Mr. Emerson about him, and Mr. William Sullivan. Depend on it, this is the way people are got into notice, by some exertions of friends. My hands are tied, and my tongue, too. Mr. Sullivan might mention [Bronson's] school to some of his friends, if he did not send any of his own [children]. I feel anxious for his success, but still feel the greatest security in his habits of industry and method.

I never felt so happy in my life. I feel already an increase of moral energy. I have something to love, to live for. I have felt a loneliness in this world that was making a misanthrope of me in spite of everything I could do to overcome it. I intend now for two years to live a third of my time at home, giving Louisa a third and you a third, and fit myself when called for to undertake and discharge with dutifulness and honor the duties of a wife.† Help me, my dear Sam, to the accomplishment of all my good resolutions, & let me hear from you immediately, before I go to Hingham which will be the nearest Wednesday, a week from today. . . . My best love to dear Lu. . . .‡ My heart is as boundless as eternity in its loves and charities. Do write me directly and continue to be to me that sincere candid friend as you always have been, the most affectionate and tender of brothers to your sister Abba.

---

*She mentions Louisa Greele, Abigail's only surviving sister; Louisa Greenwood, her adopted sister; and Mary Ann Cary May, her stepmother.

†Abigail intended to divide her time between the homes of her sister Louisa and her brother Samuel Joseph, helping them raise their young children.

‡Abigail used the nickname "Lu" for both her sister-in-law Lucretia and also her sister Louisa.

Louisa May Greele, Abigail's last surviving sister, died at thirty-six on November 18, 1828, leaving her husband and two small children, Samuel and Louisa. Three weeks later, on December 12, Samuel Joseph and Lucretia's infant son, Joseph, developed a fever and died.

To Samuel Joseph and Lucretia on the death of their baby

Boston, December [18] 1828

My dear Sam and Lu,

I have but little to say and but a moment to say that little. I can offer no consolation that your own pious hearts have not suggested already. I think I can say for myself I never knew sorrow till now. As Louisa cast her righteous eye about her and closed it upon us, I felt that the light of life had gone out from me entirely.* But the benevolent scheme of compensation came in to aid my faulting trust. Her orphans were dependent on my momentary exertions for their comfort. Her presence seemed continued to me in them. I numbered the joys of life I still had continued to me.

Oh, how prominent a figure was my little Joseph. He gave light and warmth to the little domestic circle I hoped one day to gather about me. God has laid his hand heavy upon us. I do not mourn but I must mourn. I felt a desire to see even the cold remains of my darling, but I think you were judicious in not removing him so far; he might have been injured.

The idea of passing a year in Brooklyn is very comforting to me. Make every arrangement for me and mine, anywhere so it be in Brooklyn near you, or away from Boston, the scene of complicated trial. This accumulation of sorrow is almost too much for me. I am alone but not afraid, bent but not broken. My dear Lucretia,

---

*She refers to her late sister Louisa May Greele.

your boy, your first born was, is and ever will be an angel. Love his memory, and grieve for him, for he was beautiful to behold and very comely. Who can soothe a mother's sorrow!

Sam, the pride of your heart, the joy of your eyes, has gone to Abraham's bosom. Weep!!!! There's bliss in tears when he who sheds them only feels. Dissolve the cold prospect in a flood of sorrow. It is not wrong; Jesus wept. His tear drop was his most precious characteristic. May God support you with his right arm, and sustain you by his very presence. Thomas has just handed [me] your letter—was well.

Farewell, you shall hear from me soon. My heart was full; from its abundance I have spoken, not from its intelligence. My children are well—*

Abba

To her sister-in-law Lucretia

Boston, January 3, 1829

I hardly know where to begin, my dear Lucretia, in the sad retrospect of this eventful year. The past is thrown into an oblivious shade, the future how uncertain, the present only is *ours*. You seem nearer and dearer to me than any female friend in the world, and I never needed one so much. I am full of care and responsibility, new duties, new interests, new obligations.

The idea of passing a few months with you in Brooklyn is pleasant to me, but whether we can accomplish this before April is uncertain. I was impatient with this arrangement while my sweet Joseph was there to "glad me with his soft blue eye," but that is closed upon

---

*"My children" are her orphaned niece and nephew, four-year-old Samuel Sewall Greele and two-year-old Louisa May Greele, whom she will bring with her to Connecticut to board with Samuel Joseph's family.

me. . . .* How inconsistent there are but few of us left, my dear
Lucretia. We mourn dear Louisa; there are but few such sterling
ones in this world now. Let us cling to those who are left; they will
render the journey of life more pleasant and prepare us by a fore-
taste for a purer society in a better life amid milder skies and softer
airs, where our associations will be formed by similarity of virtue
and knowledge, regardless of those connexions which are thrown
about us in this world by time and chance and which embarrass and
retard our progress on our march of existence. Let us meet; but let
us continue to act, for we can obtain rest only by previous labor!!

You mourn your son. Oh Lucretia, well you may; he was beautiful and full of promise. We can dwell only on his beautiful form.
Louisa's absence vacates the moral and sympathetic world to me.
She was ever ready to hear trouble and impart comfort. Her moral
and intellectual being was at its acme. I feel thrown as it were upon
myself.

The connection I have found with Mr. Alcott is very essential
to me. He is tranquil and firm, which you know is directly opposite to my constitution—full of emotion, strong prejudices, placable
but passionate. My dislikes are antipathies, my prepossessions [are]
loves. With this temperament how important that my future companion should be a man of judgment and decision, tranquil and
equable. He is all this, which gives me a hope that I too may one
day become what my friends may wish to have me. I do feel most
exquisitely. I give my heart, which produces emotion. It is a par-
donable sin, for it is a natural response.

But I have moral strength which restores the equilibrium, and I
go on cheerfully. . . . My time has expired. The children are clam-
orous. It is my pleasure to write you, dear Lu; it is my duty to turn
round and secure them.

                                        Farewell, yrs, Abba

---

*She refers to her little nephew Joseph May, who had just died.

To Lucretia

[February 4, 1829]

My dear Lucretia,

I never can infer in kindness from one who has ever given me real and substantial happiness. Our friendship has been an intelligent friendship founded on these principles which time strengthens and circumstances confirm. Had you never addressed a line to me I could not have inferred forgetfulness of me and my interests. We have always felt a mutual confidence founded on respect for each other's mind and sympathy for each other's heart. We have professed little, but I believe enjoyed much. . . .

How inadequate is language to convey the emotions which are excited by the contemplation of this event [a child's death]. Silence is our refuge. Hope becomes trust, confidence joy. I have three motherless orphans, all suffering for that care which a *Mother* only can give, that care which you were so abundantly bestowing on your darling.★ He is taken, they [are] left. Their mothers have ceased to bestow care and love; your child [is] removed beyond the need of yours. How mysterious!!!

My situation here has been a solitary one this winter. . . . Mr. A[lcott]'s plans are all at loose ends. [Schools in] Bedford or Hingham have the preference to Brooklyn in his mind. It is decidedly preferable to me to be near Sam and you. I shall abide by his decision. Mary-Ann [Williams, a mutual friend] has been with me a fortnight. I do love this girl. She is possessed of that moral power which can remove mountains. . . . Tell Sam his Brooklyn address [on education] was highly approved by Mr. [William] Russell, and it will appear in the next journal with three articles by Mr. Alcott, who already bears the distinguished

---

★The "three motherless orphans" in her care were Louisa May Greele, Samuel Sewall Greele, and Elizabeth Willis. "Your darling" was Lucretia's dead son, Joseph.

appellation of the "American Pestalozzi."★ This is gratifying to me. . . .

It is the golden age of improvement. "Mind" is the order of the day. People are beginning to believe as well as speculating assent to the fact that it is the peculiar characteristic of *Mind* to be capable of improvement, endless improvement. In my opinion an individual surrenders the best attribute of man the moment he resolves to adhere to certain fixed principles, for reasons not present to his mind but which formerly were. The instant he halts in the pursuit of inquiry is the instant of his intellectual decease, the twilight of his moral day. He is no longer *Man*; he is the ghost of departed man. But I am preaching instead of practicing. Do write me soon again. I wish you could come to Boston and make me a visit; it would do us both good. I should love to show you all that now remains of her [late sister Louisa] we have so fondly, so justly loved. Do give me some little relic of little Jo[seph], an apron or frock or shoe, that he has worn. . . . Ask Sam to write me. Tell him it is health to my life, and joy to my continuance. Anything, every thing is interesting to me that concerns yourselves. We are all well. We have had a fine winter. The sun has always gladdened us with his presence. Farewell, my dear Lu. [Ignore] the ills; enjoy the good of life.

—Abba

To Samuel Joseph

Boston March 15/16th, 1829

Dear Sam, . . .

I long to be at rest; the [illegible] has fatigued me beyond everything. Mr. Alcott's success is very secure, but prudence could

---

★Johann Pestalozzi was a Swiss educational philosopher admired by Abigail and Bronson.

not sanction our union [in] under a year. Thank her for the little token.★ I do not recognize the [illegible] boy, but it is enough he wore it and was pleased with it and I shall enjoy being where he has been tho' he is there no longer. I am full of engagements. . . . Lay your plan about our working and every thing that we may have nothing to do but *go*.

In haste, Abba

Journal entries

Brooklyn, Connecticut, April 20, 1829. The responsibility of this trust weighs heavy on my mind. . . .† I will exercise with the children; I will try to form a habit of cheerfulness that my mind may act with more vigor. I will try and read something every day, be it never to[o] little. I will learn to think with more method and accuracy. . . . If [the mind] is not laid out and cultivated into a regular and beautiful garden, it will of itself shoot up weeds or flowers of a rank growth.

I lament and ever shall the want of early culture. My mind, naturally active and vigorous, was left too much to its own pursuits and inclinations. Fond of reading, I devoured every thing which came in my way in the form of a book, thought little of what I read, but loved the act of reading. It seemed to take me out of myself and away from those about me. As circumstances and situation changed I had less time to myself and was obliged to mix in society. Here I made an eccentric figure. I cared for nobody, and generally left a party with disgust. I saw folly worshipped, beauty adored, and worth neglected, or what was worse, contemptuously treated. I

---

*Abigail wishes to thank Lucretia for sending her a "token," a small item of her dead son's clothing, as a memento.

†Abigail refers to her sense of obligation to care for her dead sisters' small children.

withdrew myself in a great measure, for which I was stigmatized as odd. Odd I shall probably be through life, for I shall ever condemn those forms of society which displace the substance of life.

Brookline [Massachusetts], April 27, 1829.★ I have finished reading Locke's essay on human understanding. It suggests what is important to every mental being. He looks upon the understanding as the lever of our existence. . . . The idea that moral duties are susceptible of demonstration struck me as very powerful. Every thinking reflecting mind must realize that they are perceived as it were by intuition, which is quite as convincing, though less logical. Everyone who thinks at all knows what is right and wrong. How important then that reason be cultivated early. Children, until within a few years were not allowed to think and reason. They were treated like machines, machines not active in themselves, but which were to be acted upon. Our eyes were to be blinded to this great luminary till one day be different, and we permitted to feel our way through childhood and youth. . . .

In her late twenties, as Abigail struggled to raise her nieces and nephew, she continued to try to educate herself. The deficiencies of her own education made her more convinced of the need to provide children the opportunity to think for themselves and cultivate their reason.

To her fiancé, Bronson Alcott†

> Brookline, [Massachusetts,] June 10, 1829

Dear Mr. Alcott,

    . . . A more vivid dream I never had than last night. We were in

---

★Her older sister Louisa May Greele's family lived in Brookline, just west of Boston.

†Someone in the family later wrote "Omit" on this letter.

Charles Street, I at the work table; you by my side rather dejected. I burst into tears, and in a subdued tone broke a silence I could no longer endure: "Will you forever be picking over my moral excrescences? Only have patience till I have time to recover myself. You will find me less faulty, though believe my candor when I say, if you love me for my perfections, you are loving a creation of your own imagination."

You spoke not, looked not. I ran upstairs, fell on my knees, and thanked God with as true a fervor as I ever did in waking hours that I had a feeling heart, if not a knowing head. In a moment I was by your side; my tears were smiles. You rose, embraced me most tenderly. "My dear, these transports of feeling are amiable, but unmeaning." "What," said I, "is nothing wise but what can be proved to a demonstration?" You laughed; I cried, and melted into life.

Love is a mere episode in the life of man. It is a whole history in the life of woman.

The first thought [I had] on waking, "Oh that he was this moment by my side, to what important results might this discussion lead us." But we are separated. . . .

Is it too true that love is a mere episode in the life of man. It is a whole history in the life of woman. . . . It certainly has the greatest sway. I sometimes advert to our conversations or discussions, and my fear is that I may cease to please. . . . Sometimes I think our friendship grows stronger by time and adverse circumstances; then again (it may be weakness) I fear lest absence and [illegible] occurrences may convince you how unimportant the presence of a mere woman is to you, and that circumstances may separate us till necessity becomes habit. . . .

In her late twenties, Abigail was engaged to a man without education, money, or regular employment. This troubled her father, who wrote to her in Brooklyn of his and his second wife's concerns about Abigail's choices.

From her father to Abigail

Boston, July 6, 1829

Dear Abby,

... I am perplexed [that] you have withdrawn yourself from my family, formed an engagement for your future life, undertaken a charge of responsibility, which is very great, and all and more, without asking my permission or advice. ... I can only say, she can forgive when she ought, as far as any mortal I have ever known, and of her friends and of her self, I only ask that she may be judged by her works.*

Journal entries

Brooklyn, July 18, 1829. I am often struck by the similarity of our views on most subjects.† [But] I do not build my hope of future happiness on this similarity of taste and opinion, but on the constantly strengthening conviction that we are disposed to make each other happy.

July 26, 1829. My reading has been desultory, not so much from choice as necessity. My [illegible] generally active and happy, my health indifferent, my cares have been too unremitted, as my anxiety to discharge the trust of dear Louisa's orphans has been to make efforts, the repetition of which has sometimes been too much for me. The heart is willing but the flesh weak. It was a responsibility and situation of my own taking, but like many of my plans, more perfect and desirable in design, than execution.

----

*Colonel May refers to his second wife, Mary Ann Cary May.
†Abigail is referring to herself and her fiancé, Bronson Alcott.

To her brother Charles May

Brooklyn, October 20, 1829

Dear Brother,

. . . I am a daily, nay, a momentary sufferer for that mental discipline which can alone be acquired in youth. My mind is diffusive. I have even allowed myself to wander about in the regions of fancy or imagination, and when I come to travel up the hill of science, or am obliged to contemplate the realities of life and condition, I find myself fatigued or weary without having gained by my toil, or grown wise by my contemplation. Tears fall and fast, often betray my dissatisfaction and failure. I yield to despondency, rather than conquer by perseverance. I have strong faculties but they are perverted, and the rigidity of age has placed its seal upon this deformity.

At her family's church, King's Chapel, Boston, on May 23, 1830, after an engagement of nearly two years, twenty-nine-year-old Abigail May married Bronson Alcott, age thirty. Following a party at the May house on Federal Court, the newlyweds retired to their first shared home, a room in a boardinghouse nearby. Over the next thirty years they would occupy more than thirty rented or borrowed residences.

Her father's account of her dowry

Account of sundries given my Daughter Abigail at her marriage with Amos Bronson Alcott, May 1830.

Cash, sent to her at Brooklyn,	35.
Cash, paid her at my House,	20.
Washstand . . . Looking Glass, 10 tumblers,	
12 Wines . . . 500 Needles . . . Hair Mattress,	
basin, Ewer & Chamber	12.62

Cups & Saucers, plates, bowl, pitchers, chamberpot	3.99
1 Case dessert Knives & Forks, Pail, Broom &c	2.95
3½ gall. oil, Cannister . . . 2 tablespoons, 2 dessert spoons, 6 teaspoons	16.
Cash paid at my House in part, Wardrobe	10.
Sofa, table, book rack, cart.	29.63
Repairing & Covering the Sofa, & adding Castors	12.71
Carpeting, rug, Blankets.	49.43
Looking glass frame, binding & thread	55.64
Cash paid you at your lodgings	266.02
	$500.00

Boston, 31 May 1830, errors excepted

Jos. May

Two weeks after her wedding Abigail was pregnant. The next week she wrote to her sister-in-law in Brooklyn, Connecticut. Her advice to Lucretia in regard to managing servants foreshadows the "Experiments" chapter of Little Women.

To her sister-in-law Lucretia
three weeks after Abigail's wedding

Boston, June 15th, 1830

My dear Lucretia, I had written you one of my long letters full of the spirit as well as letter of matrimony but delaying to send it by that day's mail. I kept it back in hopes to add something about a [hired servant] girl or woman. Can find no such body to be had for love or money, and your last has relieved me from a good many doubts on the subject.

I do think a *girl* is preferable to a *woman*. The latter comes to you with her habits all formed, and soon discerning how important a member she is in the little domestic commonwealth becomes a despot, for the love of power is *inherent,* I believe. And a woman without, who has intelligence to direct and benevolence to modify, is a tyrant of the worst order, for she compels us to yield our little wishes, and exacts all the small consequences which we all know require the most philosophy and patience, a philosophy which the best cultivated mind seldom acquires, and patience which physical strength and moral power can alone sustain.

I think, dear Lu, you will see the advantage of your experiment with [a servant] Lucy Ann. Let one or even two days' work, meals and all be wholly deranged by her neglect. The mortification and chagrin would impress the lesson indelibly on her mind. I feel as if your concerns would be more under your own control than if you had the whims of a woman to consult, or a city girl with her longings for Washington Street or religious peculiarities to worry her. I am delighted, my dear Lu, at the confidential and communicative spirit of your letter. It is only a consistent sequel to all your previous words and works to me, and tho' I have never really witnessed the beams of the honey-moon, yet there may have one in the heaven of my married life. Its general influences may have affected us all this time without our knowing it. I hope we may go through life infected with this lunacy.

My husband is all I expected; this is saying a good deal, for in my belief there are few who, in the romantic days of courtship and promise, do not overlook many of those essential qualifications so necessary to the support and security of rational and permanent connubial happiness. Love is and ever has been with us a principle not a passion, and I have already seen the good effects operating in our lives and conversations. My mind is gradually engaging in those subjects which have always been interesting, tho' never very present to it. It has suffered for those habits which it seems to me I must now unavoidedly acquire. I already feel the influence of moral and intellectual society constantly and exclusively enjoyed. I wish you were near me so that we might all reciprocate, and each be benefited. My husband's habits are all of the quiet contemplative kind, and I only fear that with my distaste for society in general that we shall be too apt to rest satisfied with our own society in preference to any more extensive and diffusive means of social enjoyment.

His school has diminished a good deal in consequence of families going in to the country. I hope some good salary offer might be made him ere long. It is important to him, for all financial concerns are very irksome and embarrassing to him. A salary would relieve his mind from those anxieties which are incident to the fluctuations of a private school.

Give my love to dear Sam. Tell him Mr. A[lcott] was pleased with his advice, contemplated to himself in the mirror, and thought himself not a bad looking man for the American Pestalozzi.

I shall write you again, my dear Lu, when the bustle and distraction of company are over, the ceremonies of matrimony soon subside. And glad am I, for they interfere terribly with the in (all the fashion) formalities of duty and affection. . . .

I am very well, have had but one illness since my marriage, and that I could trace to over-fatigue in the book stores and print shops. . . . My sweet Johnny [is] a good boy* and [I send] my best wishes that all the arms and smiles may be devoted to him,

Abba

---

*Samuel Joseph and Lucretia's second son, John Edward, born October 1829.

To Samuel Joseph and Lucretia
eight weeks after Abigail's wedding

July 25th, 1830

Dear Sam and Lu,

Your question shall forthwith be answered. I don't know why I have not written. I have thought of you daily, but writing has not occurred to me. My love of writing letters ceased to be before I left Brooklyn [Connecticut], and I doubt if it ever revives. There is an occasional scintillation of the old passion when I receive such addresses as yours, but at no other time. You kindly inquire for the Essay [on education by Bronson Alcott]; it has not, nor probably will, receive the premium, but Mr. A[lcott] has received a letter from Mr. Reuben Haines, one of their principal men there [in Philadelphia], which is worth a 100 dollars to a man who expects to get his bread if not his butter by the work of his brains. . . .

My husband is the perfect personification of modesty and moderation. I am not sure that we shan't blush into obscurity, and contemplate into starvation. . . .

How is my dear John?★ Tell him Sam Greele's rake is at Mr. Parish's and he may have it to help his father get in his meadow hay.† Kiss the dear fellow and tell all Lucretia's subordinates if they don't treat him with more attention and deference than any other gentleman in the house I shall send our "committee of vigilance" after them, who by the way are turning our young men inside out.‡ Every day we hear of confessions of breach of trust, fraud, theft, every species of juvenile immorality and vice. Oh, what security is there for a child's safety in the world of temptation, but that of early teaching them the *will* to do right. This is the substance of my husband's instruction.

★Samuel Joseph and Lucretia's baby.
†Sam Greele is her five-year-old nephew and charge.
‡"Subordinates" are servants.

Motherhood

In the fall of 1830, several months after the Alcotts' wedding, Bronson accepted an offer from Reuben Haines to teach children in Germantown, Pennsylvania, just north of Philadelphia. He and Abigail, now six months pregnant, moved to a boardinghouse in Germantown, where their first child, Anna Bronson Alcott, was born on March 16, 1831. Eleven days later, Abigail wrote to her brother and sister-in-law.

To Samuel Joseph and Lucretia

Germantown, March 27, 1831

I am so well and happy that I cannot resist the wish any longer to give you some actual demonstration of my strength and enjoyment. My dear Sam and Lu you have rejoiced with me in this, the safe birth of my child. Lucretia I suppose is ready with her condolence that it is a girl. I don't need it. My happiness in its existence and the perfection of its person is quite as much as I can well bear; indeed I cannot conceive that its being a boy could add thereto.

She is in good health, perfectly quiet, and is a true May for eating and sleeping. Her father has already begun a diary of her progress; should she be spared to us, it will be highly interesting both to her and ourselves. And should she be taken away we shall be glad that her early infancy was recorded. And had she not lived an hour after the pangs of birth, I still should rejoice that she had been born. The joy of that moment was sufficient compensation for the anguish of

36 hours. But she has lived long enough to open all the fountains of my higher and better nature. She has given love to life, and life to love.

The remembrance of that trying period has passed away and that most interesting of all occupations begun, the care of my child, and delightful it is. I would not delegate it to any angel. I am at times most impatient to dismiss my nurse that not even she should participate with me in this pleasure. I am very well, and fairly initiated in the mysteries of a bowl of gruel. I shall soon take the air which will convert lilies into roses and thus restore all my former charms, and perhaps a little more, add a fern to the former deficiency, for I feel completely rejuvenated, and doubt not that my feelings will affect my looks. I have an excellent nurse, good physician and delightful chamber, which for the last 10 days has been a heaven to me, or rather a scene of blissful enjoyment, a new creation. My husband has not left my room many hours since my illness, and though engaged principally at his table with his Manuscript, still his pleasure has shed tranquility on the scene. He is very happy in the little girl and I predict that wife has not diminished in value for having become a Mother. He sustains his character well dear Lu for domestic and parental excellence, inferior to *none*.

. . . I have felt a wish to tell you myself that I am a happy mother of a living, well child. If there be any in the world to sympathize in my happiness truly it is you. It is a happiness not to be communicated to every one. All could not understand the sacred, pure emotions which have filled and at times overwhelmed me. Excuse my egotism. If ever selfishness is excusable it is in a moment like this, when such new and tender ties are formed never to be broken, ties which age must strengthen, and which not even death can dissolve. Farewell—my love to all my friends in Brooklyn. And though in Germantown I have good and kind friends, kiss my sweet John Edward. Tell him to come and see his little cousin; this Anna Bronson is an amiable little bud. Perhaps she will be a blossom worthy his plucking one of these days.*

Visit with me soon. For tho' so happy in my new relations, I am not unmindful of those who mean every thing to me in the days of celibacy and sorrow.

Your affectionate Abba

To Samuel Joseph and Lucretia when Anna Alcott was two months old

Germantown, May 22nd, 1831

The anniversary of my wedding day. I will devote an hour to you, my dear Lu and Sam, looking over the past and projecting for the future. It has been an eventful year, a year of trial, of happiness, of improvement. I can wish no better fate to any sister of the sex than has attended me since my entrance into the conjugal state. Our prospects are good. I wish you could see our delightful situation, you would not wonder that we were willing to spend our last dollar to establish ourselves, in this little paradise. Imagination never pictured out to me a residence so perfectly to my mind. I thought my dear Sam you would be surprised at our application for the 50 dollars.† But I ought to have told you both for my own and my husband's reputation, that tho' we belong to the Genus generous, Order blessed spend-thrift, yet we are not so bad as that. We have property now about us worth 7 or 8 hundred dollars. We do not look upon our money as spent. It is deposited in furniture, books, and those things without which we could not live. The bump of acquisitiveness is nowhere on my cranium. There is rather an

----

*Courtship between first cousins was a common custom, often to maintain family fortunes.

†The fifty dollars was likely a gift or loan from her father.

indentation, but there is a distinction between diffusive and profusive. To the former I bow allegiance; with the latter I will claim no acquaintance.

This winter has been an expensive one, but we were not idle. We have made many valuable friends, and I believe a little patience shall fit us in possession of this world's goods, and that best of all pleasures, the pleasure of doing good. Our preparations have been extensive, but we have stood in one of debt. Previous to receiving your letter I had written to Father, made a simple statement of our immediate want of money to render our establishment sufficiently comfortable for 10 boarders, and wishing to obtain the loan from him or someone else of 300 dollars for one year. He promptly answered my letter enclosing one hundred and kindly saying that the rest should be forthcoming next month, when he should like Mr. A[lcott]'s note payable with interest in 3 equal divisions of 6–12–18 months, adding that he was not surprised that we should need some little aid at this time. It was one of his most kind and hearty effusions.

I wish all of my friends could see how delightfully I am settled. My father has never married a daughter or seen a child more completely happy than I am. I have cares and soon they will be arduous ones, but with the mild, constant and affectionate sympathy and aid of my husband, with the increasing health and loveliness of my quiet bright little Anna, with the cooperation and efficient care of my nurse (turned housekeeper), an amiable girl for a cook, a grand house whose neatness and order would cope with anything, a garden lined with raspberries, currant and gooseberry bushes, a large ground with a beautiful serpentine walk shaded by vines, firs, cedars, apple, pear, peach, plum trees, a long cedar hedge from the house to the front fence. With good health, clear head, grateful heart, and ready hand, what can I not do when surrounded by influences like these. What can I leave undone, with so many aids.

Note for Lucretia exclusively: (the "Out back"* is situated in a little thicket of cedars.) Mr. Haines presented us with 2 Bronze busts wall size for our mantelpiece, Newton and Locke. Mr. Russell's portrait and two flower vases ornament our rooms. A little old four-cornered round-about sofa, with a blue and yellow cover (very beautiful French fabric, seating and back), a neat Pembroke table, a centre ditto, and teacher's work table with 10 chairs, and a neat row of book shelves fitted into a recess and painted white is the furniture of our parlors, which were united by folding doors but which we have had taken off and made one long room. . . . It is only 7 miles from the city, and [there are] stages† frequently through the day coming and returning. Farewell, my dear brother and sister. Baby is in my lap and I am writing at arm's length. Do write us often—

Abba

To Samuel Joseph and Lucretia
when Anna was five months old

Germantown, August 11, 1831

My dear Brooklyn friends,

I know that letters from this distance cost money but money is trash and had better be spent in buying the thoughts of absent dear ones than in any other personal luxury. So be not afraid to write me a little oftener I beg. There are but few left in this world beyond my own little circle for whom I much care; and what is life, what is Heaven itself, if you do not have communion with those you love. I have every thing about me more to my mind than I ever expected in this world of bustle and business. My husband, quiet soul digging

---

*Outhouse.
†Stagecoaches.

after truth and treasuring up knowledge and experience, my babe adding days of health and happiness to her life and mine. Her progress is very perceptible and interesting; no one but her father has had the care of her for 2 hours since she was 4 weeks old but myself. I am reaping the rewards already. She has no bad habits. I keep no light at night; she sleeps tranquilly till morning, retires regularly at about 8 o'clock. I have no rules save one great one, to do what she indicates to have done, and she is so reasonable that I find no difficulty. Her real wants are so quickly satisfied that she has no time to get infractious. This is the true secret, I believe. I never go out without her, and that is seldom. My own grounds are sufficiently extensive for exercise. I put her in her basket wagon and draw her about morning and afternoon and she is pronounced the picture of health and happiness by all who see her.

. . . The Unitarians here are held in such horror as being worse than infidels.* My good house keeper told me that a lady had the wickedness to say that we were Unitarians. Said she, "Mrs. Alcott, I have disliked that woman ever since; I told her that you were as good Christians as ever lived." We pass I believe for kinder Episcopalians though we usually attend Friend's meetings, preferring the silent communion with our own souls. . . . This suits Mr. A[lcott] exactly. It is his doctrine to the letter and his practice to the life.

Do let us hear from you a little oftener. How is John coming on? You did not mention him in your last. When I read the bills of mortality my heart sinks within me at the fact that so many die under one year of age. Is this natural? Is a mother to embrace her tender offspring only to lay it in the tomb, to pass the period of gestation, sustain the pangs. I cannot think this is the course of nature. The

---

*Established Protestants such as Episcopalians and Congregationalists often viewed Unitarianism, a liberal sect only a few decades old, with great suspicion. Abigail was raised in the Unitarian church, which her family had joined in the late eighteenth century.

surplus population must be disposed of in some other way. This is no part of a mother's politics. The average number that die under one year of age in Philadelphia is 52 out of 136 . . . what a chapter for mothers; I have written you a medley. My time is a good deal occupied. I wish we could hear from you dear Lu a little oftener. Tell me about John Edward. I must know the little boy some how and at present this is the only way I can devise. . . . Give my love to all who remember me. . . .

Yrs, Abba

To Samuel Joseph

Germantown, August 24th, 1831

Dear Sam,

As Mr. Alcott does not visit you in person as he has been expecting to do all summer, I must take the next best method of reminding you that we are still here. For the last 6 weeks my Anna has been sadly sick with teething and bowel complaints and I have had 6 children in my family besides a goodly company to dine and be looked after all hours in the day.* My days have been busy and my nights restless. This you know unfits one for much mental effort; I have, therefore, permitted your last letter to lay by unacknowledged, thinking however that in August Mr. A[lcott] would see you on his way from Boston and tell you all about us. But he finds it quite impracticable. There is much sickness throughout the country and he goes out so little that I think in travelling he would be particularly exposed. . . .

The last time I wrote I believe it was about a letter from father. He answered my reply to that letter very promptly; I was satisfied. A few days since I had another long and very affectionate letter from

---

*Abigail had taken in boarders to pay bills because her husband's school was failing.

him, giving Mr. A[lcott] invitation to pass the week at our Federal Court and desiring very particularly a reconciliation between Mother and me.★ I immediately wrote to him my desire to have this effected. I wrote to Mother a respectful kind letter, and I hope the result will be favorable. The distance will favor our reunion and should we ever return to New England we shall be so differently situated that old associations would be destroyed; and I think with our past experience we should be more cautious of slight incidents leading to misunderstanding and unkind thoughts. . . .

I wish if [the] cholera subsides, you would make an arrangement and come on. Oh, much I do want to see you!! But when or how this is to be effected I know not. How long we are to remain here I know not. We do not earn the bread; the butter we have to think about. Mr. A[lcott] is suffering for intellectual society. . . . The word Unitarian has been applied to one institution and we have avoided as a pestilence excepting by a half dozen of rationals who seem to think if we are not sheep we must be goats like themselves. Mr. Haines's death has prostrated all our hopes here.† We did think his intimate friends and those who encouraged him to this experiment would have shown some respect to his memory, by cherishing those objects of fruit so dear to him while living, but so with his body they deposited also his plans, and nothing is recognized by any of them. They struggle along another season, but the profits of the summer are more than exhausted by the expenses of the winter. We have done well this summer, but our children all leave us in October and then it is a long time to live till June without any income worth mentioning, and living in Germantown is higher than in a market town.‡ We pay more for meat or vegetables here than in the City.

★"Mother" was her stepmother, Mary Ann May.
†Bronson's sponsor, Reuben Haines, had recently died.
‡"Our children" are her boarders.

I do wish you could come and see us this fall. . . . The journey is nothing after you have started. It may be the last you ever pay me.*
My love to all. We receive your paper regularly; it must do good.†
Yrs, Abba Alcott

Abigail became pregnant again before Anna was a year old, and gave birth to her second child, Louisa May Alcott, on November 29, 1832. None of Abigail's journal entries from that year survives, and most of her writings from the period before and after Louisa's birth appear to have been destroyed. Ten years later, she recalled having been "unusually" depressed in 1832, "suffering under one of those periods of mental depression which women are subject to during pregnancy."

Autobiographical sketch

We resided in Boston until December [1830] when we left for Philadelphia in company with Mr. William Russell for the purpose of commencing a system of instruction on a new and enlightened plan, in Germantown, a village about 6 miles north of Philadelphia. We continued at this place 2 years with uncertain and vacillating prospects of success. Louisa May was born on November 29, 1832. The following April an agreeable proposition was made to Mr. Alcott to go into Philadelphia to open a day school, which he cheerfully accepted, as those who first projected the scheme at Germantown were either dead or had lost their interest; and it was becoming obvious that we could not succeed without patronage and intelligent aid.

---

*Abigail is suggesting that her situation in Germantown was so difficult that she might no longer be there if her brother's family waited to visit her.

†Samuel Joseph's paper was the *Liberator*, edited by his closest friend and ally in abolition, William Lloyd Garrison.

To her father

Germantown, January 13, 1833

There is no hour of a woman's life, my dear father, when from the abundance of a grateful heart she may utter grateful things than that hour "when life's young pulse begins its mystic play, and deep affection's dreams of form, or joy, are all unveiled, a living presence to the yearning heart & fond, beholding eye." My little Louisa (hallowed be the name) is a fine stout girl notwithstanding the perils of her early existence. The winter has been favorable for her, so mild & genial; no snow or ice as yet.

As the spring approaches it brings with it its plans & anxieties or rather doubts. It seems quite settled from the results of two years experience that this is not the place for our establishment & we have exhausted our means in living to best [illegible] advantages. Had Mr. Haines lived, his efforts would have been all powerful & our risk comparably nothing; but with his death the life & hopes of this plan departed likewise. Several propositions have been made [to] Mr. A[lcott] for the city [of Philadelphia] & if they can be made secure to him we may remove there in March. But there are so many religious neighbors to contend with that a free, modest mind is confounded in its political arrangements. . . . If we go to the city my little home is broken up for we must board. This I regret, as the comforts of domestic life are best enjoyed in one's own house if it be ever so small. But I have resolved that whatever may be my destiny never to lose sight of this truth, that our happiness should not depend on the extent of our dominions but on our adaptation to our real works which are few; & under all circumstances to find pleasure in my husband & children whose lives, health & approbation are worth more to my peace & comfort than houses or lands. These are the life of my happiness and the happiness of my life.

Do write soon again; your letters are all present joys & future pleasures, so multiply them, dear father, that you may make us glad in your life, & wiser & better that you have lived.

To Samuel Joseph and Lucretia
when Louisa was eleven weeks old

Germantown, February 20, 1833

Dear Sam and Lu,

I have been wishing to write you for at least 2 months, but my eyes have been in no state to permit so great a pleasure, more particularly as my good friend Mrs Haines and [another woman] seemed to require this attention as a duty.* I knew you could hear a silence without stigmatizing it with neglect, I therefore wrote to them which cost some more pain and trouble than it was worth.

I hear you have sold your house; blessed independence. I never want a larger domain than 3 rooms, 1 servant, my husband and children for occupants. It is a thankless employment to take care of other people's children. . . .

You giving up your house seems to loosen your ties to Brooklyn, a haven that you have tilled and planted. Now do quit and let somebody else reap who are more lazy and less disinterested. . . . You are wearing yourself out for this remnant of God's people, who after all are perhaps hardly worth the effort. You ought to be in a wide field of action, in a more enlightened region of the Christian world. I find with my contact with the world so much selfishness and so little brotherly love that I am very much disposed to hug my own and revolve in as small a circle as possible.

---

*By her early thirties Abigail had developed serious eye problems, which over the years would make it increasingly difficult for her to read.

My children are thriving and are blessings indeed. Louisa May now almost 3 months old is a sprightly merry little puss, quirking up her mouth and cooing at every sound. My Anna is an active pantomime little being, loving every thing to death, and often hitting her sister from pure affection. She is round and fresh in her complexion. Mr. A[lcott] is well and as good as ever. Many women have done well for companions, but I have excelled them *all*. (Lucretia excepted). . . . What's the matter with Mother, and how are all things in Boston? Do give us your opinion of the present state of feeling; and what is going on there among our circle. . . .

Every crow thinketh her own the blackest, so I think that my babes have no sin. Do let us hear from you soon as soon as we have concluded on our removal you shall know the why, the when, and the whither. . . . Farewell, Abba, with love . . .

To Mrs. Jane B. Haines,
the widow of Bronson's sponsor

Phil[adelphia], April 9th [1833]

Dear Friend, [and] One who loves to write as well as I do . . .

The spring has arrived and since our departure from German-town, . . . we have settled ourselves snugly down at Mrs. Eaton's in more humble apartments than we occupied before, but more consistent with the comforts of a nursery, and the measure of our pockets. . . .*

---

*After two years in Germantown, the Alcotts moved to a boardinghouse in Philadelphia.

To Samuel Joseph and Lucretia
when Louisa was six months old

Phil[adelphia], June 22nd, 1833

Dear Sam and Lu,

It is a good while since I wrote to you. I write but seldom to any one, excepting father; I frequently have an opportunity to send him a line and I always improve it as I know it satisfies him to be thus remembered, and it costs me but little effort. But a full connected letter seems to me now a formidable undertaking. My eyes are very uncertain, and my time is abundantly occupied with my babies. It seems to me at times as if the weight of responsibilities connected with these little immortal beings would prove to[o] much for me. Am I doing what is right? Am I doing enough? Am I not doing too much, is my earnest inquiry.

I am almost at times discouraged if I find the results prove unfavorable. My Anna is just at that critical period when the diseases incident to her age make her irritable and engrossing; and yet so intelligent as to her making inferences and drawing conclusions about every thing which is done for her, or said to her, and I live in constant fear that I may mistake the motive which instigates many of her actions. Mr. A[lcott] aids me in general principles but nobody can aid me in the details, and it is a theme of constant thought, an object of momentary solicitude. If I neglect every thing else, I must be forgiven. I know you laugh at me and think me a slave to my children and think me foolishly *anxious*. I can bear it all, better than one reproach of conscience, or one thoughtless word or look given to my Anna's injury.

Well, dear Lu, how do you like the fair girl?★ Aren't they dear little creatures? What's her name? How I should love to take my

---

★The "fair girl" is Lucretia and Samuel Joseph's eight-week-old Charlotte.

Louisa (who is all smiles and love) and spend the day with you, and tend baby. I hope, dear, you get sympathy and care and kindness and tender looks from all about you. These are moments when tenderness and love are our best nourishment and support.

I hear that John is a 'noble boy' and has made a visit to Boston.★ Can't he make a visit to Phil[adelphia] with father? I'll take the best care of him. If I talk long about you I shall cry and then goodbye, letter, for my eyes absolutely refuse me the two businesses at once, crying and writing to you. Am just as tearful as ever when I think of the few dear ones left me on earth. But when I stick to my little family and my round of little duties I am brave and invincible as a lion. . . .

Your philanthropic friend Arnold Buffum was here, called on us, says the [antislavery] conv[entio]n was conducted with great propriety and decorum.† He hoped that you would have attended, and . . . I hope that through the colored medium we should have our eyes blessed with a sight of you. Only think, dear Sam, how quickly this journey can be made, only 9 hours from New York, and the expense is not great. . . . We have removed our lodgings to Mrs. Eaton's, South 5th St. opposite the State House square and Athenaeum. . . .‡ Mr. A[lcott]'s school promises well. Do take John and start *tomorrow*. Frederich Fry will preach for you, and for once let the dead bury their dead, for you are on an errand of charity and mercy. Mr. A[lcott] has got worlds of talk to have with you. He has got a nice little study all to himself, and you may talk over every thing undisturbed and it will do you both good to open your budget. . . .

                                                                    Abba

---

★John Edward May is now three years old.

†Arnold Buffum was a wealthy abolitionist and the first president of the New England Anti-Slavery Society.

‡The Alcotts had removed from Germantown to downtown Philadelphia, where Bronson planned to start yet another school.

Her thirty-five-year-old brother, Samuel Joseph, was now in the midst of the greatest controversy of his life, a pioneering effort by a young schoolteacher to desegregate schools. Miss Prudence Crandall, a Rhode Island Quaker, had welcomed a black girl to her private girls' school at her home in Canterbury, Connecticut, prompting most of her white students to withdraw from the school. Her neighbors smashed her windows and poisoned her well, and the town meeting voted to stop Crandall on the grounds that "once open, this door and New England will become the Liberia of America." An ardent abolitionist, Crandall decided to test the principles of racial equality and universal education by advertising in the abolitionist press a new school for "young ladies and little Misses of color." Free black families along the eastern seaboard sent their daughters to her school, which reopened in April 1833 with twenty black students. To prevent racial "amalgamation," the Connecticut legislature immediately enacted a Black Law forbidding the education of Negroes from outside Connecticut except in free public schools. Local authorities arrested and imprisoned Crandall for breaking the new law. Samuel Joseph May came to her defense, arranged for her release from the county jail, and made his parish the center of her legal strategy. At public events, where her gender prevented her from speaking, he was her representative. At her trial in Brooklyn, the county seat, he warned the prosecutor, the leader of the American Colonization Society, "I will dispute every step you take, from the lowest court in Canterbury up to the highest court of the United States." Crandall's conviction was thrown out on a technicality, largely because May and Garrison were so eager to appeal a conviction to the Supreme Court. But the violence against Crandall continued. After neighbors set fire to her house she sent her students home and moved west. But her case, which propelled Abigail's brother to national prominence, had raised the crucial question, in his words, "whether the people in any part of our land will recognize and generously protect the inalienable rights of man without distinction of color." Among the few extant letters from Samuel Joseph to Abigail is one he wrote during the controversy.

To Abigail from Samuel Joseph

Saybrook [Connecticut], July 1, 1833

My Dear Abba,

I came to this place on Saturday last with Lucretia and the children for their benefit of their health. Both John and the babe have the whooping cough.* The babe is now in the midst of it, and suffered with a good deal yet it does not wear off her flesh as I should expect it would. John . . . is now very well again. . . . Lucretia is doing well, or would be if it were not for the care of the children. She does not like to tend baby. The crying of a child irritates her nerves as much as anything.

A day or two before I left home your pleasant letter of June 22d came to hand. I assure you I am very desirous to make you a visit. All my arrangements were made to have started a fortnight ago today, but John was just then so sick I was afraid to leave him. . . .

Our affairs at Canterbury assume a more serious aspect. Last Thursday Miss Crandall and her sister were both of them arrested, tried before two justices, and bound over to the court. In August next her friends thought it best not to interpose. But permit her persecutors to do all that they would, so that the community might have a fair opportunity to judge of the temper of the men and the nature of the Law. We therefore decline giving bonds, and they therefore committed her to the jail in Brooklyn. We shall now appeal to the public to know if they *will* countenance such men and such measures. This affair I think will bring the matter to a crisis. Mr. Judson, I am told, means to publish a pamphlet that will overwhelm me, but I trust I shall have some thing to say in reply.† I am

---

*The "babe," two-month-old Charlotte May, was the first cousin closest in age to Louisa May Alcott.

†Andrew Judson, a neighbor of Crandall's, was the leader of the American Colonization Society and of her opposition.

satisfied that the questions growing out of slavery are to be the most agitated, an agitation that we have ever called up in this country. I almost dread the discussion, but it must not be waived. We have let it alone too long. And our country will be ruined, if we cannot remove the whole slave system and elevate the colored population. My mind is settled upon this point. I dare not retreat.

A few weeks ago I visited Boston, as you know, with John Edward. I found father in fine health and spirits. While there Mr. Jonathan Phillips and cousin Thomas Sewall both returned from Philadelphia, and brought the most delightful intelligence from you and your children.* We also heard from Charles while I was there. A gentleman reported that he had seen a large number of funds with his name as the inspector. How happy we shall all be if Charles does well.

Your own situation I presume from what you and others say is altogether more agreeable than you have ever been in. But I shall come and see for myself. Lucretia joins me in love to you and Mr. Alcott and the babies. . . .

We are now at Saybrook point, the mouth of the Connecticut River, this almost beautiful situation, a fine place for invalids. I am now sitting at a window from which I look out upon a large sheet of water on which numerous vessels are floating at anchor, or sailing rapidly before a brisk breeze. . . . A fine steamboat passed down from Harvard to New York, which city it will reach before sun down. I could not bear to see it knowing that if I were aboard, I might be with you [in] less than 40 hours.

Let me hear from you whenever you can write. Tell Mr. Alcott I have too much to say to him for a letter. We must have hours of talk.

Your affectionate brother, S.J. May

---

*Anna Alcott was a year and a half and Louisa was seven months old. Charles was Abigail's much older brother.

That summer the May and Alcott families had a reunion in Wolcott, Connecticut, Bronson's hometown. That fall Abigail became more involved in abolition in Philadelphia and tried to keep her brother abreast of activities there.

To Samuel Joseph when Louisa was ten months old

Philadelphia, October 1833

My dear brother,

It is quite true that we interchanged thoughts after our brief but joyful meeting at Wolcott. . . . How is Lu, and the children since their journey? Are we really to see you here? Mrs. McClellan says you are coming to wait upon her house.* Answer all these questions. . . .

Dr. Follen† has been here for several weeks, has made a great impression on some minds by his preaching and praying. He is incomparable in his devotions. Passed two hours here in philosophical discussion with Mr. A[lcott] who I guess gave him some new thoughts or at least confirmed some old ones. They are both bold thinkers—they soar high and dig deep—but such minds are somewhat solitary in this world of folly and fashion when a man's hat is the most essential part of his head, and his coat his surest passport to society.

Have you heard anything of his intention to leave Cambridge? His salary [at Harvard] does not support him. I wish all philosophers would consent to admit in their domestic arrangements a financier. They require this agent more than any people in the world. They are often (for lack of this) reduced to the most humiliating depen-

---

*Mrs. McClellan was probably a Philadelphia abolitionist of sufficient means to host the Rev. May.

†Charles Follen, a German-born Harvard professor, was asked to leave his professorship in 1835 because of his radical abolitionism.

dence. Wisdom must be fed and clothed, and neither the butcher [n]or tailor will take pay in aphorisms or hypotheses. There comes then the "tug of war" between matter and mind.

I have no doubt that you have had some *feeling* experience on this subject; therefore I need make no further comment.

Our school is slowly gaining confidence and numbers. We do not make much noise but shed some light, which travels faster and more direct, and its influence is more effective.

Mr. A[lcott] has been putting together an admirable little book of fables, allegories, emblems, parable, which if the publishers do justice to it . . . will be a valuable addition to *juvenile literature*.

How is John Edward progressing? I think much of him. And little Charlotte? I should love to be near enough, dear Lu, to help you now and then. The only way for a mother to get rest is not by cessation of labor—there is no such thing in her calendar—but by change of occupation. This I have found a great relief when I have found the burden too heavy to be borne. For tho' the heart is always willing, the flesh is *weak*. . . . In haste, yours affectionately,

In this world of folly and fashion . . . a man's hat is the most essential part of his head.

Abba

To Samuel Joseph when Louisa was twelve months old

Phil[adelphia], December 2, 1833

Dear Sam,

. . . I wrote you and asked you a thousand questions a few weeks since. Give me answers to a tenth part and I will be satisfied. . . .

Everybody is fretting about your *black* business, even the Miss Haines are "advising" on the subject. A Mrs. Johnson, a rigid orthodox Quaker in Germantown, says she is an Abolitionist from conviction. She has investigated the subject and is ready to cry aloud and share not in this abomination. I hear that Mr. Garrison has returned. What has he done? . . .

I should be willing to live anywhere where I could have one large or two small rooms, where the family are near etc. etc. . . . .

Farewell, Abba Alcott

My husband is deep in fables, allegories, parables, emblems, etc. He loves you dearly; I wish you knew more of his moral worth and power.

To Samuel Joseph when he was in New York City promoting the new American Anti-Slavery Society*

11 Dec. 1833

My dear brother, Mr. Vaughan handed me this [note about a fund for abolition], and as it may be of some consequence to you to see this gentleman personally, I thought I had better forward it without delay and to tell you that Mr. A[lcott] applied [for employment] at the post office without success. I could almost say with Achilles, "oh let me pray / the grief and anguish one abstemious day." But the cares of life compel me to press on, though a good cry has occasionally arrested my cheerfulness in the pursuit. I do realize that you have been near here, for you have opened a new avenue for sympathy and exertion.

Mr. A[lcott] thinks your progress has been great mentally and

----

*Abigail's brother, staying in New York with the abolitionist philanthropist Arthur Tappan, had been in Philadelphia the previous week for the founding of the American Anti-Slavery Society and the Philadelphia Female Anti-Slavery Society. Abigail was a founding member of the latter.

morally since you became acquainted. I tell him you were always good enough for heaven, and great enough for earth. Do give my best love to dear Lu and the children. And believe, yrs always and forever

Abba Alcott

I would fill my sheet but am fearful the mail will close and this will miss you. Do let us hear from you after you arrive home.

In 1834, with two little girls, Abigail was still in need of a stable home. For about a year her husband had lived apart from her and the children, visiting them only on weekends. While she, Anna, and Louisa occupied a series of boardinghouses in Philadelphia and Germantown, he took a solitary room near the Philadelphia Public Library. Increasingly disenchanted with Philadelphia, he hoped to return as soon as possible to Boston.

To Samuel Joseph

Phil[adelphia], Jan[uary] 19, 1834

Your letter, my dearest brother, should have been answered ere this, but various things have prevented; not the least amongst them was a dear visit at Germantown. My excellent friend Mrs. Haines desired her particular regret to *thee*. . . .* Mrs. M is very much of your opinion concerning our domestic relations.† Indeed she is so determined that we shall live for less and more to our minds that she has offered us "free gratis for nothing" two houses, one at the extreme north, the other at the extreme South. They are neat brick dwellings but in a neighborhood which in one case would expose us to a marshy expanse, and the other a thickly settled neighborhood, of those as poor, but I feel not quite as sure as we are.

---

*Reuben and Jane Haines were Quakers.
†Mrs. M may be the Philadelphia abolitionist who had hosted Samuel Joseph.

Another possibility is offered to us. If I should think it best to go to Wolcott or if you can find me a comfortable residence near you.★ Mr. Furness wishes Mr. A[lcott] to make a home with him, in his basement room. This would be an excellent thing for my husband and reconciles my leaving him more than anything else. . . .

Mrs. [Lucretia] Mott would be gratified I think to hear from you.† She is deeply and earnestly engaged in your cause. I am informing myself as fast as possible, and am interested. I have joined the Society tho' I have not attended any of their meetings. I cannot, I will not engage very much in anything apart from my children while they are so young. But I can read and think and talk. Mrs. Haines is collecting everything connected with it and I wish you would send me everything important upon this question.

That interesting Mr. McPh— whom you saw at Mrs. Mott's has become so much interested in the cause of Liberal Christianity that he wrote Mrs. M that he felt it incumbent on his conscience to pursue his preparations for the ministry no farther until he had examined controversy thoroughly, that his sectarian views were shaken to their centre.‡ She has lent him several books, and Mr. Furness corresponded with him and will keep him supplied with a regular course of theological reading. He says if we essay he shall devote his life to Abolition.

Mr F tells me [he] has written you about your [speaking] voice.§ He says you can almost work miracles with it. He says it is a treasure you do not appreciate. And he thinks you do not cultivate the

------

★Abigail was considering moving with her two girls to Wolcott or Brooklyn, Connecticut, leaving Bronson in Philadelphia, where she still hoped he would find work.

†Lucretia Coffin Mott, a Quaker abolitionist and women's rights advocate, was a cofounder, with Abigail and others, of the Philadelphia Female Anti-Slavery Society.

‡Mrs. Mott or McClellan.

§Mr. Follen or Furness.

produced tones enough. He says "if the ear of justice is ever closed to them" had been uttered in a subdued, gladdened tone it would have been overwhelming in its effect. But perhaps he told you all this in his letter. Do give my best love to Lucretia and the babies. My children are well. Louisa is a beauty. We call her the incarnation of the Spirit of Anna.*

The week you left us, there was an article appeared of vulgar ridicule composed of ignorance and impudence in which they said you ranked among the "Amalgamationists" or "Prudence Crandalists" . . .† You was [sic] a very respectable man; it was a pity that you had fallen into such bad company, for in this as in all other cases "evil communications would corrupt good manners." Do write me soon. I shall keep you informed of every thing connected with your cause. Give my best love to Mr. Benson and family and all who remember me.‡

Affectionately, Abba

To Samuel Joseph

Phil[adelphia], March 3 [1834]

Dear brother Sam,

I am glad to hear from you and hasten to write lest you should embarrass yourself with any arrangement which might be impossible or inexpeditious to me to meet. Mrs. Eaton seems determined we shall not leave her yet on account of expense. I sincerely believe the woman would keep us for nothing rather than have us go. And should my children continue well, I think we may as well remain at

---

*Fourteen-month-old Louisa May Alcott must have reminded her parents of her sister Anna at that age.

†The derisive terms referred to supporters of racial integration.

‡The Brooklyn, Connecticut, Bensons were William Lloyd Garrison's in-laws.

least for the present. Mr. A[lcott]'s prospect is good. I think there is less doubt than ever that he will have his number before long. Mrs. Morrison continues her friendly care of us and is a sister and friend indeed.

I have joined the Female Anti-Slavery society, [which has] chosen me one of the acting committee (to act I don't know what) but I have been reading for dear life, past nos. of the Liberator and Emancipator and some English publications. The Colonization society has certainly received a death blow on the head of its finances [due to] bad management. . . . Great dissatisfaction is expressed on this score in this city where generous donations have been contributed. One gentleman was in a frenzy when he read the [newspaper] item, 50 dollars for dining tables for the governor of the colony est[ablished] Liberia, when he had himself contributed largely and eats off a table, and dines all his friends at it, that cost but 12 [dollars].

Elliott Cressen returned from Washington a few days since, was enquired of what was the probability of having the deposits restored.* "Oh," said he, "my business was of too helping and disinterested a nature to attend to such trifles [that] 250 blacks are in jail waiting to be sent away, or by the 5 of March they'll be sold into Georgia if we do not raise funds to send them off [to Liberia]." I afterwards heard that some of those very blacks preferred [to] be sold into G[eorgia] rather than go to sea or into a foreign country.

Mrs. Morrison told me of a friend of hers who had been made almost sick on receiving a letter from her husband now in South Carolina who . . . found [that] a colored man, who had lived with them 19 years when she was a resident there, had since their removal been sold into Georgia to go into a cotton field. She said when she reflected on his kind gentlemanly conduct to her and her children

---

*The Philadelphia philanthropist Elliott Cressen opposed abolition and supported the "colonization" of African-Americans to Liberia.

during the frequent absences of her husband, his faithfulness to her
interests for 19 years, she could not bear the thought, and that if
money could restore him she would have him back, if she went
to Georgia herself to get him. He
belonged to a neighboring planter
who let his service for 19 years and
then sold him for 300 doll[ar]s. He
can read, write, and keep accounts.
He may prove a nucleus of free-

> *Home does not consist in house
> and land but in friends, our partner
> and children, and our mind.*

dom to those in ignorance and bondage—that good may come
out of evil here. I see good Mrs. Motte [*sic*] occasionally, and Mrs.
Earle. Her husband has made himself rather conspicuous and sufficiently obnoxious by his politics—a violent [President Andrew]
Jackson man, "tries to pray the most by inflammatory declamation."
. . . We are all well. My husband busy with and for the little folk.
Do Mr. and Mrs. Gray continue in your house? I am sorry to have
you leave that meet place, but you know your own business best.
And I have learned by experience that home does not consist in
house and land but by the friends, in our own bosoms, in our part-
ner and children, and our mind.

Do write when you can. I hear that Dr[s] Channing and Follen
were going to deliver addresses in the chamber of the Legislature
during their present session on Abolition, "*immediate* abolition."*
Is it true?

Yrs affectionately, Abba

Philadelphia, March 11, [1834]
Since I wrote you, my dear brother, much that is truly interesting has transpired and I am about to give you (which you may make
useful for your paper, if you do not obtain the same facts from a

---

*The Rev. Dr. William Ellery Channing, an esteemed Unitarian minister and
mentor of Samuel Joseph, and Dr. Charles Follen.

more intelligent source) a few facts connected with the cause of Abolition which are truly encouraging.

Last evening David Paul Brown, a lawyer and distinguished citizen of this place, pronounced a "Eulogy on Wilberforce."* The large hall, "Musical Fund Hall" (the same one you spoke in), was thronged. The Colonizationists and Abolitionists had previously furnished him with their respective documents that he might examine the subject before he gave the public his private decision. It was with breathless attention therefore that each party awaited utterance. He candidly and with great force and justice explained the origins, motives, and principles of the Colonization Society and then with the same impartiality, the views, motives and purposes of the Abolition Society. He then very eloquently discussed the merits of each, the impracticability, inefficiency, and delusive principles of the former, and then the "justice, righteousness, and safety" of the latter. For some time he was so equivocal as to leave it doubtful what would be his own individual opinion, but it revealed itself at last in a burst of indignation that we had been so long heirs of prejudice and co-heirs of credulity.

In Colonization he saw oppression in its worst form, prejudice in its ugliest feature. . . . In Abolition he found moral rectitude, divine faith, and mercy with healing in its wings. These were the weapons to root out a great national evil, a greater moral iniquity.

He recommended forbearance on both sides. Tho' colonization may have retarded Abolition, the latter should at least concede to the former a kind intention and that from their experience, vicissitude and defeat, they had learned . . . caution. . . . He concluded with a beautiful tribute to Wilberforce . . . [and mention of] one star brighter than the star in the hilt of Orion [that] shone brighter and warm in his breast; it was the Star of Bethlehem. "Go ye, my fellow citizens, and with its reflected radiance as a guide, do likewise,"

---

*The English abolitionist William Wilberforce, who had recently died, only three days after learning that Parliament would pass his Slavery Abolition Act.

with the fear of God before your eyes rather than the fear of public opinion or private odium.

I have not done it justice, but I have tried to give you the idea faithfully, tho' phraseology is a little varied for the sake of abbreviation. I believe it is a death blow to the hopes of the Col[onizatio]n Society. . . . I hope this Eulogy will be published. I will send it forthwith, with all news and papers in which its merits may be discussed. . . . I am reading for dear life. . . .

yrs, A.

In the summer of 1834, the Alcotts and their two girls, three-year-old Anna and Louisa, twenty-one months old, returned to Boston, where Bronson was to start another school. His Temple School initially prospered, but parents soon questioned Bronson's judgment and methods, and enrollment dropped, an experience he had endured in every teaching position. To pay his growing debts he closed the school and auctioned off his classroom books and furnishings. The Alcotts spent the next few summers with her brother's family south of Boston, in South Scituate, where Samuel Joseph was both a pastor and an agent of the antislavery movement.* Abigail gave birth to a third daughter, Elizabeth, in 1835, and to a stillborn son in April 1838.

To Samuel Joseph after the Alcotts returned to Boston from Philadelphia

Boston, September 1, 1834

My silence, dear brother, must have seemed almost mysterious and inexcusable, but the fact is just this. We have been so unsettled in our plans, and our prospects were so indefinable that I could not communicate anything regarding ourselves.

---

*South Scituate is now the town of Norwell, where Samuel Joseph's erstwhile First Church still stands.

Mr. Alcott has now gone to Phila[delphia], will probably pass a day with you [in Connecticut] on his return. He has determined to remain in Boston. He has taken rooms at the Masonic temple, and has about 31 children engaged to *begin* with; and Miss Peabody as his assistant.* His prospects were never more flattering, but I try to suppress all emotion but that of hope, for I have always been woefully disappointed in my expectations, and I mean this time to keep on the safe side.

My health is far from good, but I believe I shall be better as the cold weather advances. I was in hopes that in the course of affairs Lucretia and I should be brought together. And any time if she wishes to come to Boston I can make some arrangement to get her into the same [boarding] house. If she liked we could make one parlor and two chambers [for] our families. We might have many pleasant hours together. I have my children very much to myself, leaving them for an hour or two with my girl and go into the parlor for quiet or social purposes, or for a walk and after they go to bed I occupy the parlor. I wish at all events she could come and pass the winter here, with her children; Anna and John Edward could go to school together every day, with Mr. Alcott, and with our two babies and my [servant] girls we could have many quiet and pleasant hours together. Boston seems more like a sepulcher than a home to me. There are few here that I care anything about and fewer that care anything about me. My home would be everything to me this winter especially. Do *think* of it. . . .

[The] infant school kept by Mrs. Moody will never succeed, until she has quieted her nerves, or been displaced. She is doing an immense amount of mischief by her influence over those little beings. Her voice and countenance and stamp of foot is enough to make them turbulent and unhappy. I saw these exercises one day

---

*Elizabeth Palmer Peabody, an acclaimed teacher from Salem, had already taught at schools in Massachusetts and Maine.

with Sam Sewall, and it was as bad as having teeth drawn. She has no self control, and of course can have little or none over the children. I would rather a child of mine should roam the street and take her chance than be under such a tyrant. She has no more warmth or refinement than a polar bear. Mr. Alcott was shocked; ask him to describe that morning.

Do give my best love to Lucretia. Tell her she had better pass the winter in Boston with me. We will help to keep each other warm. In haste, farewell, Abba Alcott

To Samuel Joseph

September 9, 1834

Dear Sam,

I must write by Mr. Gray to let you know how finely our affairs progress. Mr. A[lcott] has 35 pupils engaged and every body I see seems pleased and excited. I hope this will be enduring as well as brilliant. Every body has there [*sic*] ups and downs; this I believe is to be our *up,* turn. . . .

Miss Eliza Robbins sent you an advertisement of her school series of reading books. I send you her Grecian History which is so full of "the pacific principle" that they ought to be encouraged by teachers who wish to instill through the medium of incidental instruction the love of peace and the horrors of barbarous war. . . . She wrote an elegant letter to be read to the "Institute" on the importance of moral education to the young, but it was committed to the censors to be disposed of as they saw fit. In all probability they are lighting their cigars with it, for they actual[ly] scoff at the idea of moral education in our common schools. I heard one man say there was no *time* for moral lectures in schools. "Thou fool!" is not an honest, judicious discipline with an obstinate or corrupt boy. [Better would be] a practical lecture to every little mind and

heart, present who thinks or feels? No classical learning, or teaching rather is the "God of their idolatry," any thing which plays
round their heads but comes not near their hearts out of which are
the issues of life.

But I believe there will be a great educational regeneration and
I believe that my husband is to be the Messiah to announce to the
world a new revelation. You will think me an enthusiast. . . . I hope
Mr. A[lcott] will see you on his way home [from a visit to Con-
necticut] which I pray may be soon and *safe*. Give him your blessing
and pack him off. My best love to Lucretia and the babies, and all
who remember Abba A.

[On reverse:] My children are importunate or I should fill
this sheet for my mind is brim full and stirring with some great
thoughts, which I have not time to define or express.

Autobiographical sketch

Anna begins to go to [the Temple] school with her father 22d of
Sept 1834. [We] removed to Mrs. Perkins's [boardinghouse at] No.
6 Beach St. Sept[ember] 14, 1835. Took into our family 3 lads, for
care and instruction. . . . Left Mrs. P[erkins's] April 1st, 1836, for
Housekeeping in Front St. [in Boston] w[h]ere we took a family
of boys to board and instruct. Finding the duties of this situation
far exceed[ing] my strength and ability, and with all our expenses
far surpassing our income, we removed at the end of one year to a
small house in Cottage Place. [We] moved from Cottage Place in
October 1838 to Beach Street [also in Boston], occupying half of a
large house with Mr. Russell's family, furnishing Mr. Alcott with a
good school-room in the same.

To Samuel Joseph

Boston, January 1835

I wrote [you] a week or two since by Mr. Garrison,* have just heard that he did not go to Brooklyn, and what became of the little packet I sent him I know not. Its chief value was a little antislavery cushion for your packet. 20 reports are in circulation about you; I hope the grand one of you nearing to us is not wholly groundless. "Waltham, AntiSlavery, minister at large, etc." The last I wish was true, for with all the force of the excellent trio now in full action and authority, I suspect there is not much effect. I mean not much in proportion to what might be. Dr. Tuckerman with his sympathy and generosity, Mr. G with his sentiment and inexperience, and Mr. B with his phlegm make but poor spiritual almoners to a suffering throng. . . .†

You thrive on moral and intellectual excitement, and here you cannot get clear of it. Mr. Alcott attended two meetings last week most interesting to the philosopher and philanthropist. The Sabbath school union and a select collection of gentlemen [met] to discuss the propriety and expedience of a church for children. Mr. Alcott's accounts were most delightful. He passed an evening with Mr. Allston at his studio in company with Miss Peabody, and last evening took tea and passed the evening with Dr. Channing, who has a project . . . in this city.‡ He is much interested in the cause of antislavery, but, but, but. Great bodies move slow, but move as he will, he never can cross the path of the lesser humanitarians who will shine and revolve in spite of him.

---

*William Lloyd Garrison had recently been married to Helen Benson by the Rev. Samuel Joseph May in Brooklyn, Connecticut.

†Tuckerman was a reform-minded Unitarian minister close to the Mays. Mr. B and G were presumably also Unitarian ministers.

‡The painter Washington Allston, Elizabeth P. Peabody, and the Rev. William Ellery Channing.

Sam[uel E.] Sewall is a warm stirring advocate, not a "son of thunder" exactly like Garrison or of "consolation like May" (as Mrs. Mott says), but there is power in his head and heaven in his heart.* And these are invincible. . . .

Tell Lucretia, I have planned in the spring to take a small house if she will come and board with us and teach me housekeeping, or we will board with her and I'll take care of her children. We'll go on Miss [Harriet] Martineau's scheme of a division of labor to make a thrifty household. Mrs. Garrison has been quite sick. We see nothing of them, for they are not get outable just now and he is seldom at his office. . . .

I have given you a queer medley, but I set down to write because I cannot help it. I was so happy at the thought the powers were at work to bring you among us. Sam[uel E.] Sewall told us of the anti slavery scheme.

Yours, Abba

To Samuel Joseph after he left the ministry to work full-time for the Anti-Slavery Society

Boston, Feb[ruar]y 22, 1835

. . . Father and mother are safely removed to their new home.† The old house is empty and desolate enough. I never want to go there again.

Did you get your keys? Uncle Sam is very much grieved that you are going to leave the dignified and respectable office of minister of

---

*The lawyer Samuel E. Sewall was Abigail and Samuel Joseph's first cousin, Samuel Joseph's Harvard classmate, and from 1830 onward a close ally of Garrison and May in Boston abolitionism.

†Colonel May and his second wife had moved from the "old house" on Federal Court, where Abigail grew up, to a house on Washington Street, Boston.

the everlasting Gospel and become an itinerant fanatic!!* There are almost as many self conceited pufferies in this said "dignified and responsible office" as any I know of. There are comparatively few disinterested philanthropists to go forward in the cause of human suffering and degradation. It is a great deal more respectable (comfortable) to wrap up in the ghostly folds of a black silk gown and preach once a week to a sleeping, gaping congregation, than to go about doing good all over this world of sin and sorrow. . . .

To Samuel Joseph

Boston, Mar[ch] 6th, 1835

I write you without delay, dear brother. Mrs. Whitney will accommodate you with either of her rooms in the 3d story, for 4 dollars a week all the time, or 6 dollars while at home and 2 while absent. . . .† We shall be delighted to have you with us. Any superintendence of your clothing or washing I shall most heartily give, making a sort of a substitute for your "wifee dear." I am sorry she is not coming but I dare say her reasons are the very best and her judgment not to be disputed. Miss [Elizabeth] Peabody is thinking of taking a room or rooms here. I anticipate a pleasant family. . . .

Mrs. Child has been to Washington and in person face to face petitioning for the pirates, to the Attorney General and the President.‡ The former treated her with the greatest politeness and sym-

---

*Uncle Sam was Abigail's wealthy uncle Samuel May, her father's only brother, who lived in Boston and would later loan her his house whenever he was abroad.

†Mrs. Whitney ran the Boston boardinghouse in which the Alcotts now lived and where Abigail hoped Samuel Joseph and his family would join them.

‡Lydia Maria Child, a prominent American writer and abolitionist, was Abigail's close friend. Child went to Washington to seek a stay of execution for the crew of the Spanish ship *Panda,* who had been found guilty of piracy. The attorney general was Benjamin Butler; Andrew Jackson was president.

pathy, the latter spurned her as a fool and madwoman, as if the decision of the President of the U.S. was to be affected by the intercession of a *woman*. And she saw the wife of the prisoners' counselor. She is always sick with disappointment and apprehension for the pirates. Jackson said all the women in the universe could not make any impression on him. He talked like a fool without brains or heart. She is a wonderful woman, a combination of the philosopher, the Madame de Stael, Joan of Arc, and all the other great in thought and action. Her character has arrived to the morally heroic.

My kind love to Lu and the children. Hope to see you soon.

Farewell, yrs, Abba

To Lucretia

Boston Apr[il] 12 [probably 1835]

. . . In most of the boarding houses they object to taking children. Some crusty old bachelor or musty old maid is amazed by their noise and protest against them. But *here,* we are very fortunate. The family consists of Miss Peabody and brother, Mr. Thomas Everett and our two families. . . .* The family are very kind and obliging, . . . disposed to keep to themselves. You and I, dear Lu, may have many happy evenings together, as well as hours of social comfort. John Edward and Anna will be at school 6 hours in the day, and Louisa and Charlotte can play together to more advantage than the older ones. I hope we shall find it so, at least my dear Lucretia you cannot continue the effort of separation from your husband without a great loss to yourself and him. He has been chosen Corresponding Secretary [of the Anti-Slavery Society] which will keep him more in Boston than he at first supposed, and I do

---

*Elizabeth Peabody, her sister Mary Tyler Peabody, and the Alcotts were all living in Mrs. Reed's boardinghouse at 34 Chauncey Street, Boston.

believe you will find J[ohn] E[dward] benefitted by Mr. A[lcott]'s mild, quiet, regular but firm discipline. He has not entirely secured obedience in his own children, but he does it most successfully for others. This is not I believe an enigma. . . .

I am not very well. My feet swell so badly that it is misery to walk, and sitting in the house so constantly almost benumbs all my faculties. My children are in fine health and spirits.

I see nothing of Pa's family. He calls at the door to leave a letter or ask for the "agent" but his daughter is not thought of, or if thought of she is not wanted, so that I do not see him.★ I try that it shall not discourage or worry me, but it is like the eternal dropping of water, imperceptibly, but wears.†

I find Miss Peabody very social and pleasant. She is very fond and sweet with children, and often keeps mine for hours interested in stories and pictures to her own evident satisfaction, as well as their delight. She is truly good. . . . She is very poor, but hopeful and resolute. She is not the first genius that has craved bread and received a stone. Her death would be celebrated in Marble and Eulogy tho' her life is almost forgotten and her peculiarities vilified and chastised. She and the minister have grand discussions and she will be an enthusiastic abolitionist before she thinks of it.‡

The agent is fine, I think, and went off most heroically on his first mission. Mr. Alcott and Dr. Channing think he has grown fierce. His spirit is the true one, unlike Thompson or Garrison; he will do more good now than either of them.§ His resolution is

---

★Samuel Joseph now worked full-time as an agent of the Anti-Slavery Society, traveling and speaking.

†Abigail continued to have a strained relationship with her father, now age seventy-five.

‡The minister discussing abolition with Elizabeth Peabody is Samuel Joseph May, who is also the "agent" in the next sentence.

§The British abolitionist George Thompson and William Lloyd Garrison were more famous than the Rev. May.

that of moral conviction, and . . . his power lies in his conviction of the truth and righteousness of his cause, and it is irresistible; his manners are so courteous and popular that he must please inevitably. . . .

Yrs most truly and affectionately, Abba Alcott

With three small children and no stable home, having to move every few months, Abigail often felt "agony, embarrassment and publicity," she confessed to close friends such as her husband's colleague, Elizabeth Peabody, and the latter's sister Mary Tyler Peabody.

To Elizabeth Peabody

August 1835

. . . If trial and friction make strong and bright, I shall be strength and brilliancy personified, in the next state of existence, for my spirit has been through all sorts of graduated furnaces in this last one . . . [I will] rise to the occasion. . . .

To Mary Tyler Peabody

Boston, September 2, 1835

Dear Mary,

In nearly a fortnight I have been hanging on the most precarious contingencies, regarding houses, leases, auctions, help—money &c—Nothing is yet concluded upon, but that patience is to do her perfect work upon me and my soul.

This reminds me (by way of Digression) of my Louisa's definition of patience. Her father was eating a piece of Gingerbread. She wanted a piece of his (having finished her own). He told her she could not have any more until afternoon, and that she must wait patiently. Do you know what patience is? said he. Yes, said L[ouisa], it means wait for ginger bread. I could not do better than that myself.

But to return to you, dear Mary, and our purposes. I mean to get to housekeeping very soon, when or where I know not, and I sincerely regret that that item is not settled that might secure your visit to us and your friend on the eve of departure. We may yet manage it in the course of next week, you shall be apprized at the earliest moment of our movements. Something like domestic and social enjoyment is in store for us I am sure this winter. I feel it in my bones (as the old woman says).

We suffer because we feel, and die because we know. Woman was told in the beginning that her sorrow should be greatly multiplied. For what? Because she desired knowledge.

I pray, dear Mary, that I may have reason to rejoice that our offspring are girls, or incipient women, but I do so dread the contact, the contamination, the conflict with the world that I almost dread a farther development of their virtue lest the suffering be the more augmented from the very contrast of that which is so evil in the world, vice in all forms and attitudes, ready to attack, molest, and make afraid.

Now Mr. Alcott would call this a horrid & skeptical and naughty kind of *assertion,* & cannot dignify it with the name of *reasoning.* But it does seem to me that on just in proportion as our virtuous susceptibilities and capabilities are developed and educated. Are we too tired and crucified? We *suffer* because we *feel* and *die* because we *know.* Woman was told in the beginning that her sorrow should be greatly multiplied unto her; for what? Because she desired knowledge, the knowledge of good and evil. But I am not a great hand at doubtful points of disputation as some wise-acre has it. But I say that I do think, and know that I do feel.

. . . My respects to your parents. I hope E. feels kindly toward me.* We do battle on the field of Colonization Spoils, but we shall shake hands over the victories of Abolition before long.† The dawn is obvious in the dark horizon, depend on it, dearest Mary. We shall live to see the perfect day. Then how those mistaken patriots will exhort the hills to cover them, and the mountains to fall upon them, and the oblivion of forgetfulness which the scorn and contempt of portend.

> *Every woman . . . is answerable to her God if she do not plead the cause of the oppressed.*

                                                                    A.A.

I mean in particular those men who desecrated Jeremiah Hall and who have tried to make the cradle of liberty the coffin of freedom. What they intended for a stumbling block will prove a stepping stone to this righteous cause.

G. forgot to send this by trunk, instead got your letter to E. & sent it to Dedham.

To Miss Mary T. Peabody, Salem, Mass.

Journal entry

January 2, 1836. It [emancipation] is a cause worthy of the best and most intelligent efforts of every enlightened American. . . . Every woman with a feeling heart and thinking head is answerable to her God if she do not plead the cause of the oppressed, however limited may be her sphere.

---

*The Peabody sisters' mother, Elizabeth.

†Abigail and Samuel Joseph were strongly committed to abolishing slavery and giving freed slaves equal rights as Americans, but most Bostonians opposed abolition and preferred colonization, removing slaves to a colony in Africa.

To Samuel Joseph May, now pastor of
the First Church in South Scituate, Massachusetts

Boston, Apr[il] 23, 1837

Dearest,

You shall certainly know the why and the where and the how very soon if you desire it. We are sweetly and quietly settled in Cottage Place, a clever little girl to assist me with the children, and I have assumed all the cares and labors myself, no deputies. . . . Everything in the way of preparing food is quite simple and unmysterious. The gridiron . . . no longer has any terrors for me and I am quite successful in my messes, or as Dr. Graham would say in my "combination of nutritive substances."* I wash once in 2 weeks for which I pay 50 c[en]ts and once a week with the aid of wash towels and little things. . . .

You have seen how roughly they have handled my husband. He has been a quiet sufferer . . . I rail, and he reasons and consoles me as if I was the injured one. I do not know a more exemplary being under trial than this same "visionary." He has more practical philosophy than half the doers who are so afraid he is thinking too much. His school is very small. . . . He will begin with about 10 or 12 [students] this summer term. I sometimes think extreme poverty awaits us. . . . But oh, my girls, what exposures may they be subjected to. But I will try not to woo doubt lest I woo sorrow, and I surely need not the alliance to wither my faith and hope. . . .

I am no angel tho' I expect to be one of these days. I never aspired to any kind of a pinion but a goose quill, and I shall be very apt to flap that about while there is anybody who cares to see my flight.

Give my kindest love to dear Lu and Charlotte and whenever you come to Boston come right here and you shall have a bed or a

---

*Sylvester Graham was a physiologist who recommended the use of his own coarse Graham crackers to maintain health.

mattress somewhere, and the pleasure of my cooking à la Graham with the Alcott improvements.

Yrs in haste, always in love and gratitude, Abba

During the 1830s, when Abigail was nearly constantly pregnant, breastfeeding, or both, she suffered several miscarriages. After a miscarriage in 1837 she recovered in South Scituate with her brother's family. Even as she submitted to the conventional nineteenth-century female role, she continued to resist the limitations that society and her husband placed on her.

To Samuel Joseph after her recuperation at his house

Boston, June 21, 1837

Tell little Charlotte I told Anna and Louisa how kind she was to their mother, and smoothed up her bed and fixed her pillows and bell for her, and they cried to think how good she was, and even sighed out the wish that she too might be sick that they could serve her in like manner.* Anna has strung her beads with intense pleasure and Louisa wishes her to accept of a pair of gloves which a friend gave her but are too small. I have a bundle which I might wish to get to you. . . .

If [only] I could feel submission, but oh! this rebellious thirst!!!!

We are in doubt as yet about all our movements. Mr. A[lcott] still has faith clear as the noon day sun. Mine is not yet as big as that grain of mustard seed they talk about. I am afraid I shall always be a doubter! God forbid I should be a joiner!

. . . Yrs in haste, always in gratitude and love, Abba

*Charlotte May and Louisa May Alcott were both four; Anna Alcott was six.

I am so pleasantly settled here I dread another change, but what is life but one series of vicissitudes, trials, sufferings, death? . . . If [only] I could feel submission, but oh! this rebellious thirst !!!!

To her husband while he is visiting Samuel Joseph's family

Boston, July 28, 1837

Nothing very special has happened but the feeling of an oppressive void which you have made in this little home. I hope you are enjoying everything. . . . Mother [Abigail herself] . . . reads a little, writes her little journal, and walks with [two-year-old] Elizabeth who is bright again and more lovely and loved than ever. Anna and Louisa are cutting the same capers, and schooling by fits and starts as usual.

A letter arrived from Sophia Peabody.* She is very anxious you should come to Salem. . . . I hope you will go to Plymouth and see Geo[rge] Bradford. . . . He may aid you in forming some plan perhaps for lecturing, or something which would give you less labor, and more money than a day-school.

In April 1838, in Boston, Abigail gave birth to what would have been her fourth child, a stillborn boy.

Journal entry

April 6th, [18]39. Gave birth to a fine boy full grown perfectly formed but not living. Mysterious little being! Oh, for that quickening power to breathe into its nostrils the breath of life to make

---

*Sophia, the third Peabody sister, an artist, later married Nathaniel Hawthorne.

it mine even for a short lease. Oh, for one vital spark of that heavenly flame to rekindle, reanimate its cold and quiet clay!!! No! Dark mystery doth hang round nothing pure, but God alone! I shall yet be permitted to read this hidden secret.

Why, after nine months of toil, a severe and tedious labour, yearning panting hope of a living son, my soul should be pierced with this sharp sorrow. I do not ask for a revelation, I know I must have it, or the needful discipline cannot be complete which my soul needs. May patience do her perfect work. May I wait, be still, pray, hope, live, watch!

To Samuel Joseph two weeks after her stillbirth

Boston, April 22, 1839

Dear Sam,

You should have been thanked many days since for your letter and [the gift of] potatoes, but I have had a sore finger on my right hand and could wield neither pen [n]or needle and am doing it now at the risk of an unusual degree of illegibility. But Mr. A[lcott] is head and ears over in copying [his book] Psyche for the press and I ask no carnal favors of him while so engaged in the works of the Spirit, although he thankfully partakes of your eat offering twice a day. . . .

Our plans are all undefined. We seem to be floating along, sometimes rough, then smooth, then becalmed, sometimes high and dry, then engulfed in our ocean of difficulties. But I am getting hardened, toughened, indifferent. I care less for this world than ever, and when for 24 hours I was balancing into another [world], I felt a serene satisfaction which I may never know again, and which I could not account for. What was it? A satisfaction in the past, or hope in the future, [or] indifference to the present?

No! It was none of these. I am not satisfied with the past; little has been done, much left undone. I have no hope in the future. The "well done, good and faithful" will never greet my ears. I may not [be] indifferent to the present for I was feeling a poignant sorrow at leaving my excellent husband, my darling children in this vale of trial and of tears. I was feeling too (as I can never describe) the cruel neglect of my father and family. What they could have produced, that calm and serene sensation at the almost inevitable prospect of leaving all . . . !!! I have been very sick. Dr. R slept here one fortnight, taking advantage of every favorable symptom to relieve me. But 2 weeks elapsed before I could be freed from the hounds and terrors of this part of the mortal arrangement. But I am again alive and active and now I beset myself to the task to find out what is to be done. Mr. A[lcott] has 4 scholars. We are very poor, and should have starved if it had not been for a few friends. Mr. A is going to Concord in a few weeks. Emerson* seems to be earnest for him, but it is a difficult case. I hope the strife of mortal things will cease ere long for I am tired and weary, and would gladly lay me down.

I hope when you come up you will come here and that we may have a chance to talk. My plans of going to Wolcott is all out for [Bronson's] Mother is going to the West.

My love to Lu and Charlotte.

Yrs ever in affection and gratitude, Abba

To Samuel Joseph

October 3, 1839

My Dear Brother,

I have been waiting for a private opportunity to thank you for your acceptable and delicious favor.† We have all acknowledged it

---

*The writer and thinker Ralph Waldo Emerson, a former minister, was a close friend of the Mays and Alcotts.

†Samuel Joseph had sent his sister a half barrel of produce as a gift.

many, many times at our frugal repasts. I sent Mrs. Child a small basket full as she was staying at Mr. Loring's and catering for herself.★ She comes in frequently to see us, and enlivens our solitude by her brilliant and joyous moods. I wish I knew the process by which her mind has made such rapid and profound advances!! She is certainly a great woman. Tell Lucretia I rather think it's coming, our [women's] turn to rule and reign; there's Miss Victoria at the head of the clan of petticoats. Oh we shall put you [men] down, depend on it. . . . I have been kicking up a dust this long time too among the dainty ones a little, but I do think in sure earnest that a great revolution is commencing, and that women are to be prominent in settling all these great moral questions now in agitation.

You ask me, dear Sam, about Mr. A[lcott]. His school is very small. We are as poor as rats. Dr. Alcott is to take half our house and we are to live on the strictest Graham principles, that is to say, not only eat saw-dust but wood horse and file. . . .† Mr. A[lcott] is of good courage; poverty presents no terrors to him. He sits around cowering with the gods. I sometimes fear in producing the life of his [spirit] he will produce also the death of his body. I have dismissed [a servant] Aline, and the tug of war has commenced. I find at night a heavy head ready for the pillow but not a faint heart. I try to keep up good cheer, and am much exhilarated in my vocation by the idea that sometime or other if I wait long enough my present situation of which just now I have "monstrous much" will become a thought, and thus transfigured, will put off its corruption, a glorious era when my corruptible

> *I do think . . . that a great revolution is commencing, and that women are to be prominent in settling all these great moral questions.*

★Lydia Maria Child often stayed with Abigail in the months after the stillbirth.
†Dr. William Alcott, Bronson's cousin, was a physician, teacher, and reformer.

deeds shall put on incorruptible thoughts. I am in the grub state, but will receive wings one of these days, by which to mount to a more congenial clime.

Where are you? Have you been to Brooklyn? How do you do and how do you like your new house? Do write me now and then. . . . Shall I not return your half barrel with some Boston commodity, with Carolina potatoes, at 3 c[en]ts a pound. Give me any direction and they shall be punctually attended to. Dear Lu, how much I wish you nearer; how much would you lighten my toils and cheer my heart. But the seal of stern necessity is set upon me, and my wishes are sure to be my curses, so I'll try to have no wants but just what fortune demands.

Yrs in love and gratitude, Abba

My children are all threatened with whooping cough. . . .

To Samuel Joseph
on Louisa's seventh birthday

Boston, November 29, 1839

My dear brother,

. . . I wish you all a pleasant thanksgiving. May you have a turkey as big as an oxe [*sic*] and a plum-pudding as big as the brown hawk opposite my window. Should this occur I shall expect a wing of one and a slice of the other, as I do not expect to see any-thing less greasy than a hard [baked?] Carolina potatoe [*sic*] or boiled rice. Oh, those physiologists!! may their bowels never yearn as mine do for pick-bones and cranberry sauce!

Early in 1840, increasingly dejected over his professional failures and inability to support his wife and children, Bronson moved the family from Boston to a rented house in Concord, where he hoped to farm and write. Three months later, on July 26, 1840, Abigail gave birth to their fourth daughter, Abigail "May" Alcott.

To Samuel Joseph

Concord, April 26, 1840

Dear brother,

. . . The children and I have a flower bed. And we mean to look gay before long. I shall depend much on your visit. The children are well and joyous all the day long; Anna goes to school and thinks Mr. Thoreau another 'father' in his manner of teaching. Give my love to Lucretia and the children and believe me yrs

most affectionately, Abba.

Louisa, age seven, was sent to Boston to stay with relatives for more than a month around the birth of her baby sister, Abby May. It is likely that Abigail wrote this note to her second daughter during that period of exile from home.

To Louisa

At the cottage [in Concord], n.d.

Your sweet fragrant note, my dear Louisa, has made me happy; more sweet and fragrant was your tender love for your Mother than any odors of the nosegay. I have put them with your dear father's posy in my journal. I have placed a kiss on your lips. May they never open but in kind words and sweet sounds for us all. Blessings on your dear head, and may God be near your heart always, prays

Your Mother

To Samuel Joseph a month after the birth of Abigail's fourth daughter, known as Abby May, Abba, or May

Concord, August 30, 1840

My dear brother,

... 11 days after my confinement I was established in my household traces, dragging and pulling for dear life. Louisa Windship came and served a week, and Elizabeth Wells 3 days, and I then felt that all was going well.*

My baby is a sweet little creature and the children aid me a good deal in the care of her; Anna assumes a thousand little responsibilities concerning her and Elizabeth is full of tender care.† Louisa serves me in the way of dishes and cleaning as better suiting her genius.

We have "taken" them all from school have given up butter and milk and are trying to see if we can live on the productions of our own land and by curtailing still farther

I feel like a noble horse harnessed in a yoke, and made to drag and pull instead of trot and canter.

our expenses try to live without money or debt. Mr. A[lcott] can earn nothing here but food, and what more we need *must* come through grace or charity. The world is all of *want* before us; where to choose.

The claims of my children keep me from despair. But I feel sometimes as if life was more of a toil than was good for my peace of soul or health of body. I experience at times for whole days the

---

*Louisa Windship, a daughter of Abigail's brother-in-law Charles Windship, and Elizabeth Willis Wells, a daughter of her late sister Eliza May Willis, assisted her after the baby's birth.

†Anna, Elizabeth, and Louisa Alcott were nine, five, and seven years old, respectively.

most exquisite sense of weariness. I cannot get rest. I feel like a noble horse harnessed in a yoke, and made to drag and pull instead of trot and canter.

Then again, I say, well if I must go . . . I will try to go patiently; the burden may be never so heavy but it is the steady pull and strong pull that gets it off at last. Mr. Alcott would like a more peaceful movement by an animal without Spirit [that] is a mere automaton and must be commiserated for its lack of life rather than lack of grace. Our crops are doing well and have proved beyond a doubt that there is faculty and skill in the famous right hand. If it would pay our rent and give us shoes and bread we should not have to ask charity or receive advice. . . .

My constant prayer is increase my faith, for I am groping in an ocean of mysticism, and all my past experience crushes every dream of hope. I do not see, and I cannot know. Mr. Alcott is thinking of some employment for the winter. Can you think or suggest anything? Do keep him in mind and among all your host of acquaintance something might come by your only stating the case that Mr. A[lcott] is suffering for *lucrative* employment in which the principles of justice and righteousness are not involved. Consult Sam Sewall or Mr. Quincy; he seems very friendly.* My hands are tied. I have furnished a good many pairs of shoes and paid many little debts with my needle. I can do nothing now for a year at least, and Mr. Alcott must try to do something as productive with his pen. Do think of him in this connexion. And try to think of me in any other connexion than as a supplicant for aid. I would sometimes be thought of as other than a beggar.

Yrs, Abba

My love to Lu. Tell her her visit did me worlds of good; tell her my hopes all wear petticoats.

---

*Samuel E. Sewall and Edmund Quincy were wealthy first cousins of the Mays.

To Hannah Robie,
her cousin Samuel E. Sewall's aunt

Concord Sept 13 1840

Dear friend,

You need not be particular to look up a reason for writing to me. . . . Everything seems to stand still or hang by the eyelids just now, and I can neither take nor give satisfaction. We are thinking hard for occupation this winter. Mr. A thinks of taking a district school. . . . I wish people thought half as much of a man's life and bearing to his neighbors as they do about some wrinkle in his creed; but it always has and always will be so. When our friends ask, "Why stands Mr. Alcott idling all the day," I tell them, "No man will hire him." It is a hard life for the reformer; a harder one for his little family, for they have none of the eclat or sympathy for their sacrifices either now or as a posthumous comfort to sustain their hopes and endurance. But we will trust that better things will come for all of us. . . .

To Samuel Joseph★

Concord Nov[ember] 15, [18]40

Dear Sam,

I have tried several times to write you, but could not get the right pitch, sometimes too high, sometimes too low, never expressing or conveying the true condition of things. So I have successively burned the paper, waiting with all due patience for the proper mood of mind and color of soul to "shadow out" the *reality* (if there be any).

————————

★Someone, probably Abigail, later wrote on the envelope of this letter, "Pathetic—burn the whole."

But the fact is that the "don't-carism" philosophy has been invidiously creeping into my creed for the last year or two, and I am becoming perfectly indifferent to a class of subjects that once filled me with either hope or despair, love or hate. I think when it is perfectly obvious that Satan pencils against you, why it's as well, perhaps better, to suffer and grovel if it makes you more comfortable of heaven and all good influence are about you, why enjoy them with all your might and main.

I am sick of all the reasoning; it does not alter the fact, and facts are just now what I am most concerned in. A baby, cooking-stove, broomstick, and needle are facts so substantial that I need no argument from heaven or earth to convince me of their reality.

I should pronounce it all plain heavy prose but for baby who is such an angel of goodness embracing us all with her wings, one of love and one of smiles, that I am included to think that there *is* some *poetry* in life. Some music in the pestle and mortar of it makes her laugh; something in a fire blaze makes her eyes sparkle. My children are very real with their sorrows and their joys. These I supply if I can and sympathize with if possible that life shall bring no doubtful terrors to their young hearts just yet.

Thank Lucretia for her pretty frocks. They will be very useful. . . .

Yrs ever, Abba

To Samuel Joseph when her daughters were nine, seven, five, and under a year old

Concord, Jan[uar]y 24, 1841

Dear S,

It is a good while since we have interchanged letters. I am so weary with details, with private grievances, public wrongs, personal insults, new propositions, communities, expediencies, hopes, fears, heav-

ens, hells, improved methods of living, old and even poetical ways
of dying, young men and maidens, old men and children, church,
state, Holy wars (but not holy soldiers), all sorts of things. I say I am
so weary that I take my baby and turn my back to the window and
annihilate for the time every thing but my husband, children, cooking stove, workbasket, and the Dial.★ Indeed I have got into such a
mill trot that if anybody should ask me the way to Boston I should
say it was in the oven, or if I had read the last Liberator I should reply
it wanted darning, or if I had seen the account of the Groton Water
works, I should be very likely to reply [that] the children drank
them, or if I had read the Baptism of Pochahontas [*sic*] I should say it
was not brown enough. I really have no vocabulary for a letter.

Mr. Alcott is writing a series of Delphic letters which if people
will deign to read will do more for their souls than Paul or Pliny,
Junius or Jack Downing. Mr. Emerson seems fuller in the faith than
ever that [Bronson] *is the man* which is to do us a great work in these
days of sore tribulation. I suppose Anna or Miss Robie have told
you of his noble offer to us: half his house and storeroom free, Mr.
A[lcott] to work with him on his land, and I to share the household
labor with Mrs. E[merson]. The families and tables [would be] separate, [using] the same oven to bake our puddings, the same pot our
potatoes, but—tell Lucretia—*not* the same *cradle* for our babies. But I
cannot gee and haw in another person's yoke, and I know that every
body burns their finger if they touch my pie, not because the pie is
too hot, but because it is mine, and you know by sad experience that
I had a "kink" always < (improved method).

But to be serious, for my time and paper are spending, we are as
poor as rats or as church mice (and as *good* too).†

★The *Dial* was a journal of Transcendentalism, edited by Margaret Fuller.

†The remainder of this letter is cut out of the bound volume of Abigail's letters
in the archives at Harvard. The mysterious < may suggest an amplification of
her "kink."

To Samuel Joseph when he was in poor health

April 4, [18]41

My dear brother, . . . It is this dependence on others which is the worm gnawing at the vitals of my tranquility. I often say to my troubled spirit, Peace, be still, all the essentials of life are common property; earth, air, fire, water, are the commonwealth, and the owner of these can never die. But I find the wicked inventions of men have so far appropriated these that fuel must be *paid* for, water must be *paid* for, the land out of which we would dig our bread must be *paid* for. What is to be done? Must we too embrace some device to get money that we may live? We must, or starve, freeze, go thirsty and naked.

Now, dear Sam, this is no romance or rhetoric. I shall wait a few months and if I find that Mr. Alcott be leaving home of a week or two to occasionally earn something and if I can get sewing for the summer, with what aid you or any other friend can give us without impoverishing yourselves; I shall remain here. [I would] Send Anna and Louisa to [stay with] Miss Thoreau, Elizabeth to Miss Russell, and [live] with the severest economy. . . . By the fall my babe will be more out of my arms, I shall have more liberty of action and tho' I may adopt some scheme of life giving me more labor, if it make me independent of the charity of my relations and friends it will give me life indeed, and my children will not have to reproach their parents with idle words.

It is this dependence on others which is the worm gnawing at the vitals of my tranquility.

My girls *shall* have trades, and their Mother with the sweat of her brow shall earn an honest subsistence for herself and them. I have no accomplishments for I never was educated for a fine lady, but I have handicraft, *wit,* and *will* enough to feed the body and save the

souls of myself and children. As it regards the list,★ strike out one
bedstead, one mattress, pillows, and pillow cases; all are necessary
to our comfort, but not our existence, and I ought now to think of
the latter not the former, in all my considerations; the plated lamps
my heart yearned after, and father's shaving pot (the old one), but
those too I can do without. . . .

Do take care of yourself. One word of dietetic advice: substitute
black tea for coffee during the spring and summer months, [have
a] generous breakfast and dinner but very light supper. I am sure
you will not be bilious, no flatulence, and an intellectual energy
which you cannot enjoy with your present habits. You will pardon
my plain words and charge it to the account of the reforming atmosphere that I live and breathe in from all quarters of the globe, and
believe me with affection and gratitude your sister and friend,

Abba Alcott

*Abigail had to find a way to support her family, a responsibility her husband
could not fulfill. She envisioned sending her older girls out to board, which
might enable her to seek paid work as a seamstress, although she still had a
baby in arms. Around this time she sent ten-year-old Anna to stay indefinitely with Hannah Robie, who lived in Abigail's cousin Thomas Sewall's
house on Morton Place in Boston. Homesick, Anna demanded to return
home.*

★This was a list of May family possessions to be shared among the siblings. Her
father died in February 1841, leaving his estate divided into seven equal portions, of
which Abigail would eventually receive one.

To Hannah Robie

[Concord, c. 1841]

My Dear fr[ien]d,

I am quite disappointed that Anna could not forget home long enough to make herself comfortable, but it is so natural that I cannot find any fault with her want of resolution. Will you do me the favor to send her bundle with her umbrella and crash mittens★ to the stage office, as it contains her only change of thick drawers, and the weather continues cold. I am afraid to let her put on her summer ones. Please direct the bundle to "A.B. Alcott" to be sent without delay to the White Cottage over the Wooden Bridge, and it will come direct. I am sorry to trouble you but she has no other change of clothes, and do write me a few lines. Our furniture is all attached and I [am] just waiting for the next rupture of all my ties here. I had hoped that Anna would have been spared the trial of seeing the dismantling [of] the house but perhaps it is as well she should be early minded to suffering in this sad pilgrimage.

Yours ever, Abba Alcott

Concord, August 4, 1841

My Dear friend,

. . . I have been vigilant in inquiring for [employment] opportunities, desiring of all things to send my father a specimen of transcendental farming.

Have you anything pleasant to read? Your [Samuel] Johnson is on my mantelpiece, and has enriched many an hour with his profound wisdom. . . . The Rambler never tires . . .† One word is as good as half a page of modern stuff; I shall give it volume after

---

★Coarse linen mittens.

† *The Rambler* was a 1750s English periodical by Samuel Johnson devoted to morality, literature, and religion.

volume a place in my work-basket, to refresh my languid mind, or to rouse my drowsy thoughts, or to dissipate doubtful fears while at my work. If you have an old copy of [Andrew] Thomson's Sermons I should be glad to borrow it.

To Samuel Joseph

Concord, March 9th [1841 or 1842]

My dear Brother, I have been sadly busy among Father's papers, amassing them to be bound as an inheritance to my children. I always valued his words of wisdom, but they now are as rubies to me and will be a rich possession to my children. I return you a letter [written by our father] which I had filed away amongst mine. I suppose I had affixed a peculiar value to it as he spoke of me in tenderness and confidence. The letter is yours. The thought is now my own and will be cherished in fond remembrance. Yrs ever, Abba

Fragment of an undated letter to her brother Charles

You fear you shall never be married. I do not despair of you, dear Charles. We may yet have those about us who may call us father and mother. You, I believe, have known the Sex more than most of your kind, who believe that ignorance is her safeguard. Fools! . . .

They would keep her in subjection, that is the point. Surely the vocation of woman is one in which strength of mind is required to answer its demands with cheerfulness, complaisance and intelligent fidelity—the happiness of man and the education of offsprings.

> *Alas! the mind of woman is trammeled and attenuated by custom, as her body is by fashion.*

But alas! the mind of woman is trammeled and attenuated by

custom, as her body is by fashion; little mental effort is expected of her; little therefore is made. It is an error of education that perverts these omnipotent attributes; and that is why [Alexander] Pope said that "woman's life / Was a youth of folly / And an old age of cords."

The fact is, they seek diversion because they are not taught the luxury of thought. . . .

Journal entries

August 1841 . . . Why are men icebergs when beloved by ardent nature and surrounded by love-giving and life-devoted beings? Why [does he] so much take, take, [and] so little Give! Give! Women are certainly more generous than men. Man receives, enjoys, argues, forsakes. Man reasons about right. Woman feels right. Love is with her instinctive, eternal. With him it is pastime and passion.

Oct[ober] 8 [1841]. My 41st Birthday, celebrated by my husband and children in the presentation of a p[ai]r of scissors from Anna, a penknife from Louisa, a picture from Elizabeth and the following emblems and note from my husband. . . . What treasures these [are] to a wife and Mother. Expressions of love from my children and manifestations of increasing confidence in my husband.★

12th October, Concord, [18]41. Great Anti-Slavery convention. Mr. Garrison and Brother Sam[uel Joseph] passed the night with us. Had a long discussion on the merits of the Providence people; they are bold invaders of the conservatism . . . of the present age. It is easy to say to those who would pluck the beard of the hypocrites and false prophets "stand off for we are holier than thou," but it is hard to show by the life and conversation that to "do the will of the father" is their meat and drink.

★Abigail started to write "children" but crossed it out and wrote instead "husband."

Just been reading Dr. Ripley's funeral sermon.* In an extract from a memorandum he used to keep of great events in life, he says, "I have serious objections to a Diary to be inspected after death, even if it could be kept with exactness and truth. What is bad in me, why should the world know further than it observes? And if there be any thing good, by the grace of God, will not the daily exhibition of it be the best evidence to the world."

I entirely agree in this thought of Dr. R[ipley]'s. If a diary is true it must record much that can be of little use to the writer after it has occurred, and no service to the recorder at any time. If the diary is only partial it gives a very imperfect notion of the life *lived*; I have for many years been in the habit of keeping a book like this, in which I occasionally write, [but] to keep up a train of interesting facts or any thoughts which may be exercising my mind. But I could not compel myself to write every day. It would be formal and insincere, and my life has been one of no great episodes or adventures. It has been sufficiently varied by joys and sorrows to discipline my soul for moderation in success and resignation in defeat.

December 19, 1841. My children are beginning to be objects of great solicitude to me. I feel sometimes as if great obstacles had been thrown in their way especially to arouse my own energies and bring out and confirm the great and the good in them. They are fine girls [with] strong characteristics, which will be felt in society before many years. Their habits are promoting of health and intellectual strength. They are not overworked in any direction and their life is varied by innocent liberties, which give them great individuality and frankness. They are generous and fearless. They can boast of no great accomplishments; but they are in no wise deficient in any track of knowledge absolutely necessary to this age. Anna is nearly 11. Louisa is 9. Elizabeth 6½. Abba 1½.

---

*Ezra Ripley, a longtime minister of Concord's First Parish Church, was Ralph Waldo Emerson's stepgrandfather.

Early Middle Age

Journal entries

[Undated.] I value this Journal of 1841–42 more than any subsequent one, because it was a period in my life more full of hardships, doubts, fears, adversities; struggles for my children; [and] efforts to maintain cheerfulness and good discipline, under poverty and debt, misapprehension and disgrace. *Heroic.*

Jan[uar]y 1, 1842. Passed the day as usual in the interchange of courtesies appropriate to the New year. This month passed very pleasantly in my little cottage home with all the domestic comforts which few wants and small income can give.

Several English admirers of Bronson's educational theories had written to invite him to visit them in England. Ralph Waldo Emerson, his friend and now neighbor in Concord, offered to pay for Bronson's voyage. On May 17, 1842, Bronson sailed for England, leaving Abigail and their four daughters, ages one, six, nine, and eleven, in the Concord cottage with Bronson's unstable younger brother, Junius. Abigail's much older brother Charles, who had returned to Boston after decades away at sea, also lived with her and the children in 1842.

Feb[ruar]y, 1842. Visit Boston on account of my friend Miss Robie's sickness. Saw many of my friends, received some testimonies of their regard for my dear husband and children.

Mr. Alcott preparing for his voyage across the Atlantic. I dread and yet desire this separation. He requires this change of all things the presence of his Transatlantic friends. Their sympathy and future correspondence will be of importance to him.

Weaned my baby (finally) and she is in perfect health.

March 29th. The anniversary of Father's death. His life was one of great industry and benevolence.

March 6. Mr. Alcott in Boston visiting some friends previous to his leaving for England. How grateful is sympathy to his solitary soul. He wanders to and fro on the face of the earth not like Satan to destroy, but to seek and save mankind. Should he be engaged on the other side of the Atlantic in carrying forward his fledgling scheme of Education I would willingly forego his presence *here,* tho' I sometimes feel as if it were robbing my dear children of their birthright to thus separate them from their father's daily influence and the fostering care of his gentle Spirit. Could I be more free from household duty I feel as if I could make this absence at least of no loss if not some gain to them and myself. As it is I must so modify and arrange my labors as to meet the demands, with cheerfulness and zeal, that this important period of the lives of these dear children shall be blest to them in *health* and *innocence.* . . .

But oh! How great a task is this. It is with fear and trembling I undertake it. It is with a trembling hand I take the rudder to guide this little bark alone. It is with doubting heart and feeble trust that I seek for some sheltered nook, where safe from the storms of adversity, and the rude blasts of defeat I may put in with these tender babes. Faith!!

But let not indolence or timidity lay their flattening unction to my soul. Let me not cease to act, through the fear of not doing enough. I am only required by the strictest code of my religious and maternal duty "to do that which my hand findeth to do," and then with every grateful acknowledgement for blessings on my efforts, or patient and cheerful resignation in defeat, I can render my account of stewardship with a firm trust that my sentence will be one of *mercy* if not *approval.*

March 1842. Reading to the children to their great delight [Mary] Howitt's rural life in England. It carries you without locomotion right into the houses and bosoms of a beautiful world, so quietly, without all the circumstances of 'Steamers' and 'railroads.' Their customs, festivals, are very pleasing, . . . so serenely simple. . . .

Great mortality among children this winter. I can scarcely forbear to reproach parents, Mothers in particular, for their stupid inattention to the dietetic habits of their children. They regard sickness as cropping from mysterious Heaven, "alike on the just and the unjust," instead of tracing it most generally from their own habits, tables, firesides. But through much tribulation they may understand the minute anatomy of the human system. They will seek for the cause of all this sickness, and death. They will at last find that it is safe to be temperate and *simple* in the quantity and quality of their food. They will counsel them to *moderation,* as they would counsel them to withhold from slow, but surely operating poison. . . .

Waldo Emerson⋆ and many other interesting children have been cruelly torn from our midst by disease. . . . Great errors in education, modes of living, feeding, clothing, bathing, exercise, sleeping, some one of these essentials of life, wholly or partially neglected, the mind over-worked or not exercised enough. Children [are] alienated from their houses by our present School system. Their rights [are] all invaded by parental selfishness. I am surprised that they are as good and patient as they generally seem with so much that is false and factitious about them.

April 1, 1842. Enjoyed for the last few weeks in serving for Mrs. Savage and preparing my husband's wardrobe for his voyage. The time draws near for our separation. I am summoning all the important and agreeable reasons for this absence and amongst the most

----

⋆Waldo Emerson, the five-year-old son of Ralph Waldo and Lidian Emerson, had recently died of scarlet fever.

weighty is the belief that these trans-atlantic worthies will be more to him in this period of doubt than anything or anybody can be to him here.

Wife, children, and friends are less to him than the great idea he is seeking to realize. How naturally man's sphere seems to be in the region of the head, and woman's in the heart and affections. I am sure I shall be sustained in the absence by my maternal duties; these cannot be postponed or laid aside for a more convenient season. I do not love my husband less in his absence, but I love my children more. . . .

May 1842, Wednesday morn. Rose early, began the duties of the day with more than usual goodwill. How elastic is the nature of woman. She rises higher in her inward capability as she is defeated and overcome by outward circumstances. She rules fate itself by her *will*. The essential oil of seeds is obtained only by pressure; so woman to yield the intrinsic worth of her soul must be bowed down by the weight of accumulated exigenc[y], to give out the full force and intrinsic power of her moral might.

May 6. Mr. Alcott leaves us this day for Boston, expecting to sail tomorrow or Sunday for England, in the ship *Rosalind,* furnished by his benevolent friend Emerson with all the means to accomplish his voyage and visit to England. Noble friend . . .

May 7. Rose early, feeling sick and sad. The morning bright but cold. Bathed all over in cold water, scrubbed with the flesh brush, felt better. No appetite. After going by myself and weeping most hysterically, I put on my hood and walked away a few minutes. I uttered one audible fervent desire to an Almightly Providence: "Increase my faith!" . . . Must we be robbed of our treasure to know its real value? Let me improve by this great, this heavy discipline.

Sunday, May 8. Rose early, bathed, scrubbed, prepared my children's breakfast. Felt no appetite to partake, but a great desire to write, so excused myself from the meal and came to record the burden of my mind. "A fire meeteth extinction before it will yield to be cold." When the frownings of fortune are the darkest and human effort avails nought to avert its evils, where but in solitude do we find comfort, or feel the intrinsic wealth of our own great souls? If we have much sensibility, communication with our friends avails nothing; living contemplation alone stirs up the divinity within us, and we go forth refreshed and strengthened, to do, and to bear; "Arise my soul, stretch every nerve and press with vigor on"; be not discouraged tho' trouble comes like an armed man to assail thy peace. God and goodness are *invincible*. Guard every avenue to sin; thy vigilance shall make thee invulnerable.

Monday, 9th . . . I will hope all things, believe all things.

Tuesday. A busy day, washing, ironing and visiting my sick neighbor, Mrs. Haynes. Passed the evening in talking and singing with my children. Retire early.

I can think now with more composure of Mr. Alcott's absence. My thoughts begin to dwell on the fact of his arriving safely, and the desire for letters. Is not sorrow, all sorrow, selfish? Some flowers give out little or no odour, until crushed . . .

Thursday we all rose early, Uncle Junius taking the children [on] their accustomed walk. God educates children in the morning by harmonious and joyous sounds, sweet odours, and incense from every flower and dew drop.

Leave thy bed, dear child, *early,* that you may breathe *in* divine influences, before the busy scenes and cares of life divert you. . . . Converse with God, the Giver, of all the beauty you enjoy, the love that animates your young health.

Friday. The Liberator informs us that the [antislavery] meeting in New York went off finely, the subject of the disso-lution of the Union was not broached,

> *Some flowers give out little or no odour, until crushed.*

there was no great excitement, Garrison did not go. Is he not timid? Fear not, great man. Truth is an invincible shield. Faith in thy cause will pluck thee from every burning or deposit thy ashes in immortal urns.

Sunday, May 15, 1842. A week this morning since my husband left his native shore, seeking his new friends the other side of the Atlantic. The voyage will have many novel charms, the storm and calm, sunrise and sunset, noon in its glory, and midnight in its firmament of brilliant worlds, its northern coruscations, the world and all its appendages . . .

Monday . . . This friend of mine [Miss Morrison] has always been a generous believer in Mr. Alcott's motives, if she has not always felt perfect confidence in the practicality of his schemes.

Tuesday. Passed the afternoon with . . . a few of the neighbours. How little real sociability among this class of people. It's the last new frock, or new such-a-one's Irish girl, or everything that is temporary and unimportant in the Salvation of body or soul. I never meet such people that I don't think what *will* be their heaven. Certainly there must be caps, green tea and sponge-cake or it can be no heaven for them . . .

Wednesday. Received an encouraging letter from brother Sam.

Thursday, May 19. Received a very kind letter from my Uncle Sam, sending me likewise a draft on the Bank for 100 dollars my father's bequest to me. This will enable me to pay up our bills, mostly in Concord, and relieve the people here of a doubt . . . about ever getting their money. . . .

Friday. Spent in preparing my children's summer frocks and thinking much of my dear husband. I am wholly sustained by the confident assurance that this excursion was the one thing needful to sustain the just balance of his mind. Dearest! best of men, I ought to know that you will live here in the confidence and reverence of your age, as well as in the remembrance and eternal honor of posterity. . . . You shall be crowned now with laurels, that watered by the dews of divine life shall bloom in immortal verdure. Few know you now, but there are those coming up to the true perception of all that is divine and sublime in your principles and life. Patience, yearning soul!

Saturday. Passed the morning in the village paying bills [for rent, shoes, wood, milk, apples, bread, potatoes, corn, sundries, wagon rides, stationery, and stamps]. . . . The Concord people ought to thank me for circulating so much among them. I hope they will use it as righteously as we have, for the real wants of life. My legacy could not have been better applied.

Sunday, 22nd. Sabbath of rest for the body. . . . Even the sun comes up to the sky as if he knew it means a day of universal rest, as if there was a pause in the workings of the world. The earth looks new and beautiful as on the day of its creation, but it is as full of rest as if it drew near to its close.

[It has been] 12 years today since I pledged my life in the presence of the world to my dear husband. My love was plighted 2 years before. These have been great years for my soul. Wise discipline, circumstances the most diversified, have conspired to bring great energies into action. I have not been always wise, or prudent; I have looked too much to consequences, not enough to principles, and motives. But I feel encouraged. Defeat has given me strength. . . .

I am the only one of 4 sisters, who has been spared to 12 years to her husband and enjoyed the privilege of seeing her children beyond their babyhood. Oh, may my dear daughters live to feel that it has been well for *them,* that I have been spared to them yet a little longer. During the absence of their father I have an able and judicious counselor and friend in them. Uncle Junius, always cheerful, amiable, and patient, he meets all their little wants so lovingly. . . .

Saturday May 28th. 50.00 from Brother S.J. May. This will make me quite independent of our Concord debts, and with great economy I can live for very little during Mr. A[lcott]'s absence. Economy shall be my study. . . .

May 29. Three weeks today since Mr. Alcott sailed. . . . I am trying to get accustomed to the thought that I can do without him. I think I can as easily learn to live without breath. . . .

June 1. Beautiful weather! June seems never to break her pledge. . . .

Sunday, June 12. Have been reading over Mr. A[lcott]'s journals. I never have felt their full value so much as since he left us. . . . The one for [18]28, '29 records his experience in love! How much I lived with hopes chastened, soul subdued; my affections have been deepening and strengthening as his character has developed and all our souls have been merging with the lives and progress of our children. Anna, Louisa, Elisabeth, Abba, are so many epitomes of my life.* I live, move, and have my being in them. I have not much mind for knowledge drawn from other sources. . . .

June 20 . . . Junius returns from the post-office with a letter dated "June 1st, two miles from London," from my husband. . . . Now can I think of him as greeted by friends and coadjutors, surrounded by elements of kindness and love, no longer as exposed to the tempests of wind and water.

June 24. Elisabeth's birthday. We have celebrated it as usual with a few companions and a little festival, draped the Corn Barn with sheets and green boughs, which when lighted looked very lovely, vases of flowers standing about and their supper table neatly spread. How easy is childhood satisfied when the hearts of those about them are gently inclined to make them happy, a few green boughs, a few nuts and fruits are worth all the rich confections and fine apparel of the rich and proud. Father being absent they read this sentiment followed by eating a piece of birthday cake:

---

* Abigail later crossed out "Abba" and replaced it with her youngest daughter's preferred name, "May."

Father dearest
We wish you here
To see how gay
On this birthday
We are;
With flowers rare
And children fair;
There met to eat
In Corn-Barn neat
Our simple Treat.
Nuts, figs, and Cake—
I'm this day Seven
And nearer Heaven
Each year I live,
Oh may I give
A promise sure
While I endure.

Mrs. Emerson and several of our neighbors called and were delighted. . . .

26th. Wrote Mr. Alcott. Find it difficult . . . I have so much to say and the feeling that I must economize seems to impoverish my thoughts. I want to say all I think all I feel but the right words don't come and so I lose the thoughts.

27th—29th. Baby not well, requiring constant care, but I shall seek no foreign aid but trust to God and my own efforts to restore her. I am sure he will not forsake me in my doubt; "hope on, hope ever" is my motto now.

While Bronson was abroad, Abigail spent a morning at Concord's Old Manse with her friends Elizabeth Hoar and Henry David Thoreau, who were readying the mansion for the expected arrival of the newlyweds Nathaniel Hawthorne and Sophia Peabody Hawthorne.

July 8, Concord. Passed the morning with Elizabeth Hoar at Dr. Ripley's old mansion house, sweetly fitted up for the reception of Mr. Hawthorne. A charmed spot, the sweetest arrangement of the simplest articles of finest taste: Etruscan vases, antique flower-stands of old roots of trees exquisitely surmounted by baskets or boxes for flowers.

I left this scene of enchantment for once dissatisfied with my home. I have ever felt that with Mr. Alcott's ideas of beauty we have suffered for want of room. We have always been too crowded up. We have no room to enjoy that celestial privacy which gives a charm to connubial and domestic intimacy. I have suffered in my tastes, and encroached on the rights of my husband and children by this intense proximity.

I am enjoying this separation from my husband. It is giving me his soul and heart in the full melody of his rich words, even more fully than in the grand diapason of his sweet voice and the rich deep harmony of serene looks. I feel lonely; at times my solitude seems insupportable, but his letters fortify me to bear the latter cheer-fully and meet the demands of my family with swift duty. I am not unhappy. Why should I be? I know that God is near to me. . . .

[Bronson's] last letter dated 18th of June reached me the 6th of July, [containing] a sweet drawing of his residence or the Alcott House, Ham Common, Surrey. He found Mr. Greaves [his English sponsor] not living; this was a sad disappointment. . . .

Hamilton and Louisa pass the Sabbath with me, are engaged in the holy relation of partners for life. . . .* The discipline which vacil-lating hope and fear may have given her has no doubt chastened her expectations and modified her views of the connubial relation. . . . She is well prepared to bear the keen adversities which may occur in this fluctuating system of things. . . .

----

*Her nephew and niece, Hamilton Willis (son of Eliza) and Louisa Windship (daughter of Charles Windship by his second wife), were soon to be married.

July 21. Letters from A.B.A. today per *Acadia*.* He does not forget his home, though surrounded by those spiritual affinities which he has so long desired to enjoy. No, dearest; in the midst of joy you do not forget those who have so deeply participated in your sorrows. It is your defeat which has nerved me up to do and to bear. It is your life [that] has been more to me than your doctrine or theories. I love your fidelity to the pursuit of truth, your careless notice of principalities and powers, and vigilant concern for those who, like yourself, have toiled for the light of truth.

July 26, 1842. We have had a fine day at the Cliffs.† Uncle Junius took us all, being Abba's birth day July 26, into his little boat Undine or Water Spirit and rowed up there; we enjoyed it highly. We [brought] up a cake, bottle of milk and some currants. After landing we picked berries and mixed them with our sugar and a fine bottle of water, and we spread our plaid cloth under the trees and made a fine meal. Then I wrote a few lines to be sung or read as the jingle would permit, as follows:

> *River and trees*
> *Soft summer breeze*
> *Cake and flowers*
> *In Nature's bowers*
> *All meet to prove*
> *How much they love*
> *Baby dear*
> *Were Father here*
> *We'd work no more*
> *So rich a store*
> *Of life and love.*
> *Then when we've quaff'd*

---

*A.B.A. is Bronson, whose letters from England arrived by ship.
†The Cliffs are along the Concord River. It was Abba May's second birthday.

Our milky draught
And eat our cheer
Of fruit and cake
Our boat we'd take
And "Undine" fair
So fleet and rare.
Homeward bound—
All safe and sound
We'll safely go
A merry Show,
On this birth day
With Queeny gay
This day enrolled
2 years old.

I am no poet, but this jingle sometimes pleases my children who, like babes of a larger growth, are pleased more with sound than sense.

I seldom omit these occasions for showing my children the joy I feel in their birth and continuance with me on earth. I wish them to feel that we must live for each other. My life thus far has been devoted to them and I know that they will find happiness hereafter in living for their Mother.

. . . Before my Louisa was born I was suffering under one of these periods of mental depression which women are subject to during pregnancy, and I had been unusually so with Louisa which accounts to me for many of her peculiarities and moods of mind, rather uncommon for a child of her age. United to great firmness of purpose and resolution there is [in Louisa] at times the greatest volatility and wretchedness of spirit. [She has] no hope, no heart for anything, [and is] sad, solemn, and desponding. [She has] Fine generous feelings, no selfishness, great good will to all, and strong attachment to a few.

To Samuel Joseph

Concord, 1842

Dear S.,

I want if possible to have Charles settled before they [Bronson and his English friends] get here, as both he and Junius must be displaced immediately for Mr. Wright, as they can be only temporary sojourners, and he is to be a permanent issue.* Charles has a favorite plan of going to New York. If there is anything in anticipation from the Boston Estate for me, if it is but 5 dollars, I would gladly give him all to promote any object for his welfare.† It is only an aggravation to hold out broken reeds for him. He must have a strong staff a little while to give him a chance to feel his own weight, recover his perpendicularity, and then if he does not walk uprightly and freely he will have nobody to blame. . . .

Journal entries

August 2. Letters from my husband to day. He seems quite ready to return. He says, "I shall leave here nor spend a moment, gadding and gaping at the many shadows of men with which this Island abounds; I shall bring the living along with me, [Mr.] Lane and [Mr.] Wright, when I come. . . ."

August 22. The children have been decorating their father's miniature with all sorts of everlasting flowers from the Amaranthus to the field Chrysanthemum. Thus would they emblem the endur-

---

*Charles May and Junius Alcott were living with Abigail in Bronson's absence. Henry Wright was one of the Englishmen soon to arrive; the other was Charles Lane, who brought a son Louisa's age.

†The estate was that of her father, Colonel Joseph May, who had died on February 27, 1841, at eighty.

ing nature of their love for this dear absent father. . . . My letter of yesterday per *Brittania* will probably be my last, as Mr. A[lcott] had then gone to London to make his arrangements for sailing. I was relieved that his friends Mr. Wright and Lane were not to accompany him. It seemed premature, more particularly as we are not favorably situated here for any experiments of diet, having little or no fruit on the place, no houseroom, and surrounded by those whose prejudices are intolerable.

Mr. Emerson was greatly apprehensive that Mr. Alcott had dipped his pencil in Rembrandt's pot of gay coloring, and that his friends would find themselves in a barren field with no sun to cheer them, and no shade to shelter them. He says, "Mr. A[lcott] lives in such a region of high hope, that he does not feel the atmosphere of less elevated humanity, who are perishing in the chills of a cold and selfish world, or who are bullied into extreme forgetfulness of others, by their excessive interest in themselves."

All this may be true, but the resources of the great Ruler of the Universe are not so scanty or so stern as to deny men the privilege of free-will. All of us can carve out our own way, and God can make our very contradictions harmonize with his solemn ends. . . .

With what trust has my husband felt that this great idea, which has filled his mind and at times occupied his whole being, would be actualized! Is it not about to be realized? In his Journal of '38 he says: "I know that some mission awaits my faculties, and the days shall bring this to light. What have I to do but wait and watch? My hour shall come."

My children during their father's absence have looked to me to umpire and [be] sole arbiter and have been more docile and patient. The new influences which await them will bring out their great traits and confirm their good ones. . . .

Baker's life of Pestalozzi is full of deep interest. It is essentially a Mother's book, and no less essential to children. His principles, despite his failures, have since continued to spread and to reform education, even where his name was unknown. *Love* was the fundamental principle, the active agent, the ruling motive of his system of education. But all our institutions are based on selfishness; how then can we develop love in our pupils? I know of no more effective remedy, no more powerful lever than by beginning with our own family, with our own *selves*. We can do little toward reforming individuals, or society, or remodeling Institutions, while there is any lack of this divine principle in our own lives and conversation.

Sunday, August 28. Raining, dreary day out. We will have life, light, and joy within. I am daily expecting the return of my husband. I hope his home will not have lessened in his interest; I know it cannot, for my *own* experience has often taught me that duty, home, offspring are the world to a parent. This dear companion has had a weary and solitary sojourn thus far in life. . . .

What a union of [us and] these dear English friends will effect is an interesting problem now before us to solve. Can Mr. Wright do what this dear Father can not do?* At present the children are doing very well, furnished with a few simple and harmless materials. They manufacture their own employment and recreation, and learn to derive more satisfaction and pleasure than they have ever done by suggestion. "They live and move and feel that they are happier than they know."

My children may not turn out wits or *beauties,* but the monopoly of happiness is not engrossed by beauty nor that of a virtue by genius. A docile child will seldom be found to want understanding sufficient for all the purposes of a useful, a happy, and a pious life. If I do but plant and water the true seed in their hearts, God *will* give the increase. If I share not my efforts to do right for them, my labour will not be all in vain.

---

*Abigail doubted that adding to her family, such as her husband hoped to do with Wright and Lane, would improve their lives. His experiment in "consociate" living would be carried out a year later at the Fruitlands farm.

August 29 . . . Why is melancholy opposed to duty? Why do I feel such a desire for personal liberty in the morning especially, when I am encumbered with many cares, much manual labour? I am more aspiring in the early morning. . . . The soul seems more receptive then of God, and his works as manifested to us in the creation. It is perhaps because my life is not sufficiently inward, self dependent. I am too susceptible to external influences. . . .

September 4. Letter from my husband per *Caledonia*. I rather expected himself, but he did wisely to stay longer if by so doing he can secure more friends to his purpose. He speaks of several as manifesting an interest in their movements. . . .*

September 8. Been to see the Hosmer place at Stowe in reference to its capabilities for our united scheme of life.† Find the place on many accounts agreeable tho' not well arranged for chamber room to accommodate so large a family. Should think a place nearer Boston and yet more remote from neighbours more agreeable for such a plan of life. And yet place can affect individual life but little. Close my shutters and give me quiet and heaven is very near, wherever I may be situated. My mind to me a kingdom is. Give me intellectual freedom and exception from much bodily care and I shall live and thrive. The prospect of a union with those divinely disposed persons is very agreeable. We have been thrust out of our sphere and compelled to frantically move in the orbit of others and harmony could not ensue, distraction of purpose, restless inactivity, morbid action and dissatisfaction.

At Bronson's request, Abigail visited several farms for sale, seeking the right spot for the utopian community he aimed to create with his English friends.

----

*Here she transcribed a Longfellow poem, "The Rainy Day," which opens, "The day is cold, and dark, and dreary. . . . "

†Their "united scheme of life" was Bronson's idealized consociate family.

September 16. Visited the Codman farm in Lincoln, found it admirably calculated for a large family associated on terms of good fellowship, very fine house, 260 acres of land, 50 acres wood lot, quite retired from the world but accessible from the great road leading to Boston, and near the contemplated railroad. But I dare not dwelt long on any place 'till I have seen these persons. Let me see them safely across the ocean and I shall be content with anything. Whether my capabilities for such an association is at all equal to the demand I know not. My powers of adaptation to circumstances have usually been found sufficient to sustain me comfortably to my self and agreeably to others. My children I am sure must be benefitted. If *they* are, surely then am I not injured, for they are the threads wrought in the texture of my life, the vesture with which I am covered!!

September 18. Been preparing my cottage for the reception of my husband and his friends. I would have him find his home swept and garnished. The lord of our home and life shall find that his servants and lovers have not slept or idled during his absence from the field of labour. We have toiled and shall reap the harvest of his "Well done! good and faithful!" This is all I could ask, all he can give, to fill me with joy and content. . . .

[I am reading] "Metaphysical Mothers" by Miss Peabody.* There is nothing in true education which has not its germ in the maternal sentiment, and every mother would find more of the spiritual philosophy in her own affections, if her mind would read her heart, than could be obtained by years of study in books.

Oct. 8. This day I complete my 42d year. This has been an eventful year. The two extremes of deep anxiety and high hope have met, the one to try my *faith,* the other my *fortitude*.

Passed the afternoon on the 'Cliffs' with my children. Brother S[amuel]. J[oseph]. and wife passed an hour with us at supper. Received a [birthday] note from Anna, Louisa and Elizabeth.

---

*Elizabeth Peabody.

We always notice these occasions. Had dear "Father been with us our joy had been complete" was oft repeated by the dear children who associate his presence with all occasions of supreme happiness. The love instinct of childhood seldom errs. The gentle influence of this dear father is powerful to charm and cheer at all times. We find no substitute for it. But dear little ones, let us not love each other less, because we love father more. We will be all in all to each other, and every thing to him.

May gentle gales, and gentler waves, bear him and his dear treasure of lives and loves home to us, safely. May no dangers affright them, no perils assail them. Hold this precious casket, God, as waters in the hollow of thine hand! till time and occasion replace its jewels in the regalia of our Cottage home. . . .

On October 9, 1842, Abigail pasted in her journal a schedule of the British and North American Royal Mail Steam Ships on which she marked the schedule for the Britannia, *sailing August 4 and arriving September 1, and for the* Caledonia, *sailing August 19 and arriving September 17. She wrote on it, "Come!" and addressed it to A. Bronson Alcott, Alcott House, Ham Common, Surrey. She pasted nearby a picture of a woman pouring water and wrote, "The Spirit of health, of joy, of good, Prescribes water for Drink, and plain bread for food."*

October 21. Good news for Cottagers! Happy days these!! Husband returned accompanied by the dear English-men; the good and true.★ Welcome to these shores, this home, to my bosom!

Sunday, October 23. After dispatching the duties of the morning, walked with friends and children. I was deeply impressed by Louisa's ebullition of feeling. "Mother what makes me so happy?"

★Bronson arrived with Henry Wright, Charles Lane, and ten-year-old William Lane, who all moved into the Alcotts' cramped, rented cottage.

[Louisa asked.] Mr. Lane relieved me from replying, for a big prayer had just then filled my heart, and stifled utterance. I wished to breathe out my soul in one long utterance of hope, that the causes which were conspiring just then to fill us with such pure joy might never pass away. The presence of my dear husband, the gentle sympathy of kind friends, and the inspiring and exhilarating influence of nature; who so longingly embraces us . . . that we soon find ourselves wrapt in heavenly vesture and while contemplating the material we are imbibing the divine elements. I have had an abiding confidence during Mr. Alcott's absence, that he would return safely. I had an assurance that *his* righteous enterprise, and my patient trust would not be defeated. I knew that a reunion of spirits would be vouchsafed to us, that "love divine all love excelling," would crown our later days, and hope and happiness be meted out to us more abundantly than hitherto. We have planted and watered in our natural life, may we reap and garner in a divine love.

November 29, 1842. Mr. Alcott's and Louisa's Birth-day, passed as usual in the interchange of little gifts. Circumstances most cruelly drive me from the enjoyment of my domestic life. I am prone to indulge in occasional hilarity. But I seem frowned down into stiff quiet and *peace-less* order. I am always suffocated in this atmosphere of restriction and form. Perhaps I feel it more after this 5 months of liberty and option. My diet too is obviously not enough diversified, having been almost exclusively coarse bread and water. The apples we have had, not being mellow, and my teeth very bad, my disrelish for cooking so great that I would not consume that which cost me so much misery to prepare.

All these causes have combined to make me somewhat irritable, or morbidly sensitive to every detail of life, a desire to stop short and rest, recognizing no care but of myself seems to be my duty. And yet without money we can do nothing. I urge myself on from the consideration that this seems but a state of transition, and that instead of rest I only need a different mode of action. And so I wait; or rather plod along rather doggishly.

I hope the experiment★ will not bereave me of my mind. The enduring powers of the body have been well tried, the mind yields, falters, and fails. This is more discouraging to me than all else. It unfits me for the society of my friends and my husband and my children. They all seem most stupidly obtuse on the causes of this occasional prostration of my judgment and faculties. I hope

Give me one day of practical philosophy; it is worth a century of speculation and discussion.

the solution of the problem will not be revealed to them too late for my recovery, or their atonement for this invasion of my rights as a woman and a Mother.†

Give me one day of practical philosophy; it is worth a century of speculation and discussion . . .

Abigail's birthday present to Louisa that year was a pencil case and a note that read in part, "I have observed that you are fond of writing, and wish to encourage the habit. Go on trying, dear, and each day it will be easier. . . ."

December 24. Left Concord [for a visit to Boston with Louisa] to try the influence of a short absence from home. My duties for the past three months have been arduous and involved . . .

Sunday, 25. "Christmas day." How full of association. To me anything but merry!! Went to the Episcopal church in Roxbury with the children. . . .

★The "experiment" was Bronson's utopian dream, soon to be realized at Fruitlands.

†Louisa later wrote beside this entry, "Poor dear woman!!"

Fragment of an 1842 letter to Samuel Joseph, most of it excised

. . . it seems to me that it has been in my darkest hours that my soul has emitted the brightest powers, and just in proportion as the outward has failed me, the inward has developed the all sufficient for strength. . . . If we cannot do great things the good ones will be more worthy.

Journal entries

Sunday, January 1, 1843. Returned last evening from Boston, glad to resume the quiet duties of home and love. How the satisfaction to a heart and mind constituted like mine, is all the circumstance and show of society. How little is the social compact understood or felt. Is it not one tissue of selfishness, fraud, and corruption? I left home toil-worn and depressed. I returned feeling quickened by a new spirit of confidence and love. I received a note from my husband during my absence. One thought I will preserve here as another illustration of his perfect truth in God and goodness. He says, "I sincerely believe that you are in the arms of a benignant Providence, who shall do for yourself and us, more than we can conceive or ask. Let Him guide, relinquish all self-willfulness; be willing to be used as he shall direct. . . ."

January 4. I am quite absorbed in my mental condition. Felt since my return from Boston an unusual quietude, less tenacious of my rights or opinions. I do believe that the miracle is about to be wrought. To be truly quickened into spiritual life one must die a carnal death.

January 11, 1843. Read aloud to the children. Quite a happy day, [they] thrown much on their own resources and I upon my own reflections. Freedom of thought and action is indispensable to my happiness, and consistency of action, restraint, uncertainty, doubt, is paralyzing and destructive to my mind and heart.

Sunday, [January] 15. Established to-day a household Post-office. I thought it would afford a daily opportunity for the children, indeed all of us to interchange thought and sentiment. Had any unhappiness occurred it would be a pleasant way of healing all difference, and discontents. It is to be opened every evening after supper and the letters notes or parcels to be distributed to the respective owners. A budget basket hung in the entry is the receptacle for all communications. No child or person is to open the budget during the day. But the post-master is to do so and distribute in the evening, each child taking turns to be post master.

March 6, 1843. Preparing notes and little tokens for the Post office. This has proved a very agreeable arrangement for domestic intercourse.★

March 6, 1843. Went to Lexington to pass the day with Brother Sam, in the hope that he would suggest some means of paying up our little debts before leaving for our new establishment. He seems quite at a loss himself, and feels dissatisfied that Mr. A[lcott] finds no means of supporting his family independent of his friends. They have to labour, why should not he? It is a difficult question to answer. I leave it for time to settle; his non-willingness to be employed in the usual way produces great doubt in the minds of his friends as to the righteousness of his life, because he partakes of the wages of others occupied in this same way. It certainly is not right to incur debt and be indifferent or inactive in the payment of the same.

Sam is much embarrassed how to proceed, with no means to help us himself, and no confidence in the disposition of others to do so. *"Dependence is the life of a Spider,"* hanging by a thread, invisible.

★Abigail's family post office later inspired the household post-office scene in *Little Women*.

Note to Louisa, age ten

March 12, 1843. DEAR LOUIE . . . I enclose a picture* for you which I always admired very much, for in my imagination I have thought you might be just such an industrious good daughter and that I might be a sick but loving mother, looking to my daughter's labors for my daily bread. Take care of it for my sake and your own, because you and I have always liked to be grouped together.

By the spring of 1843 Bronson had secured financial backing from Charles Lane to begin his experiment in "consocial," or communal, living, apart from the world's corruption. Lane purchased for the community a farm in Harvard, Massachusetts, with a mortgage that Abigail had persuaded her brother Samuel Joseph, who had no more money to donate, to cosign.

On the first of June, Lane, his son, William, and the Alcotts moved to the farm, beginning the famous Fruitlands experiment, which Louisa later satirized in "Transcendental Wild Oats." In a letter to the Dial, *Bronson and Lane described the community's austere rules, including bans on meat, milk, cotton, and any other product of capitalism or slavery, and a general distrust of marital sex and the conventional nuclear family. Abigail assumed full responsibility for housework and cooking at Fruitlands, with the help of her elder daughters, while Bronson and Lane sought money to fund the community. The first payment on the mortgage would come due in November.*

Journal entries

Harvard June 1, 1843—Fruitlands. This day we left our little Cottage House at Concord after a residence of 3 eventful years. During that period my Abba was born; my father died; Mr. Alcott went to England, returned with his friends Lane and Wright. Mr. Lane with

---

*An etching of a mother and daughter.

my brother purchased this estate which I hope will prove a happy home. If we can collect about us the true men and women I know not why we may not live the true life; putting away the evil customs of society, and leading quiet exemplary lives. Our labour for the present must be arduous, but there is much to strengthen our hearts and hands in the reflection that our pursuits are innocent and true, that no selfish purpose actuates us, that we are living for the good of others and that tho' we may fail, it will be some consolation that we have ventured what none others have dared.

To Samuel Joseph
soon after arriving at Fruitlands

Harvard, June 14, [18]43

Dear S.

When I wrote you last week, I thought I was to go by Mr. Wyman and that as I had but a few moments I would not attempt to describe our place and its environs. I had much to say but was fearful I should not say it well or quite truly. But lest you should for one moment be under the apprehension that I am dissatisfied, I hasten to discharge your mind of any such misapprehension. The house is even better (shabby and ill-looking as it is) than I expected, for they described it as being scarcely tenantable, whereas I assure you if all God's creatures were as well sheltered as this, there would be no suffering on this score. The land is reported to be admirable; we have already planted that which may yield 500 bushels of potatoes and the men are going on finely. Abraham and Larned are with us, and a hired man works on the place. Woods, groves, pastures, brooks are delightful and as to the prospect it is indescribable. An interminable range of lofty hills "whose summits pierce the heavens as with a wedge," green undulating escarpage, whose [prospect] is oppressive with wonder and delight. Our children are very happy and when the planting is over we shall establish a school. Now if we can attract towards us a few of the right caliber I do feel as if a great work may be effected here. The true life *ought* to be lived here if any where on earth, away from the false and degrading customs of society as now fashioned; apart from observation, no ambitious motive stimulating us to a false action. We may fail, but it will be something that we have ventured what so few have dared. We have had two beautiful Sabbaths, so much repose without, and holy quiet within. I am charmed with the solitude of the place. . . .

But you must come and make your own observation of the outward and the inward shall be faithfully reported from time to time. We have not taken the horse or wagon, therefore instead of stopping at the village of Harvard, tell the stage driver to leave you at Mr. Edgerton's this side [of] Still River village, and some of us will be over to get you . . . It will only be a mile, across the fields. . . .

I meant to have acknowledged receipt of the $5.00 [you sent]; it came and was a great comfort as I paid of[f] all my little scores and we owe *nobody nothing,* [have] our own wood and no searching for meat or potatoes. It is a comfortable feeling after a perturbation of 10 years.

Mr. Lane seems very happy and Mr. A is in his element . . . fidgets about the dirty house, but as that is my element we are quite comfortable. Love to all. Tell Lucretia her love is more substantial than the world's Gold. I have proved its true metal [*sic*].

Journal entries

June 25 1843. A sweet quiet Sabbath. Yesterday was Elizabeth's birthday, which we celebrated in the woods. . . . We prepared a Bower and placed on a small pine tree some little gifts and notes, a little quarto called "Daily food," a fan, a little pitcher, and silk

Balloon for a cotton spool, also a pincushion. After trimming the halls with oak leaves we took breakfast as usual, then repaired to the Bower. Mr. Lane taking his violin we sang a few songs, then read the notes some . . . in poetry which I will insert. . . .

From Mother

Lizzy my dear
We are here
To make you smile
And pass awhile
With song and flower
In this sweet Bower . . .

On the Pine—
A gift of mine
You'll find;
Now be kind
And excuse
This poor muse. . . .

That summer, in addition to traveling to collect new members for Fruitlands, Bronson and Lane visited local communities of Shakers, a religious community that banned sexual relationships and procreation. The two men were drawn to Shaker practices, and both considered joining the Shakers.

2d July. Reading as usual from 10 to 12 o'clock.

Mr. Alcott most beautifully and forcibly illustrated on the black board the sacrifices and utter subjection of the body to the Soul, showing the † on which the lusts of the flesh are to be sacrificed.

Renunciation is the law, devotion to God's will the Gospel; the latter makes the former easy, sometimes delightful. Pure resignation elevates and illuminates life. Sweet peace already fans the air near this my cross:

> *Then round about the starry throne*
> *Of him who ever rules alone,*
> *The heavenly-guided soul shall climb.*
> *Of all this earthly grossness quit*
> *With glory crowned for ever sit*
> *And triumph over Death, and thee O Time*[*]

July 18. Sam[uel Joseph] and family pass the day at Fruitlands, Harvard, Mass.

Monday . . . I did not think so much curiosity could have existed among our friends to see our new home. . . .

> *Shame on the world! In madness or in pride,*
> *Has woman's mental birthright been denied.*
> *Be she the weaker; kindly give her might;*
> *Be she man's equal, then it is her right. . . .*[†]

August. A busy toilsome month, somewhat relieved by the air and presence of Miss Page, an amiable active woman whose kind word and gentle caretaking deed is very grateful to me.[‡]

Mr. Alcott and Lane visit Boston. Mr. A returns quite sick, continues quite feeble.

---

[*]The verse is a paraphrase of a portion of Milton's poem, "On Time."

[†]The quatrain is by Frederica Bremer, whom Abigail admired.

[‡]Ann Page was the only other woman who stayed to live at Fruitlands, amid an expanding collection of men.

To Samuel Joseph from Fruitlands
in late summer 1843

Sunday Noon

I hasten to write and to thank you from my heart for all your kind sympathy.

Dear Sam,

When I wrote on Sunday Mr. A[lcott] was low indeed, nor did I see by what human aids he was to be restored. When I added my P.S. on Tuesday the acuteness of his disease had passed, but he still seemed to me not essentially better, and the means he permitted to be used were to my mind wholly inadequate, but he was constantly saying "Thy *faith* shall heal thee."

My common sense was stronger than my faith. I insisted on [a diet of] spearmint tea and a total abandonment of vegetable food, blackberries, . . . shower bath twice a day, and the most living faith you ever witnessed has indeed restored him but not made quite whole this dying man.

On Friday he went with Mr. [Thayer] to the Shaker Village and spent the day in conversation. He was too feeble for it, and has been more nervous and excitable. On Saturday William Channing came for a few hours, was much struck with the alteration in Mr. A[lcott], his sepulchral tones, and extreme languor. . . . Beard Palmer and son are passing the Sabbath here.★

He [Bronson] sees too much company his mind is altogether too morbidly active. I thought of proposing to him a little quiet journey in a chaise, leaving the children with Mr. Lane and Abraham,† but

---

★William Henry Channing, a poet, was the minister's nephew; "Beard" Joseph Palmer was a local farmer.

†Abraham Everett was a local cooper.

he says no and he wants rest, perfect quiet "that when he journeys it will be a long one—and *alone*."

I do not allow myself to despair of his recovery, but Oh Sam, that piercing thought flashes through my mind of insanity, and a grave yawning to receive his precious body would be to me a consolation compared to that condition of life. Don't mention this to even Lucretia or Elizabeth.* It may be owing to his extreme debility. I am encouraged to find him overcoming this terrible diarrhea so entirely. His system was more healthfully active than I had supposed.

The Cattle are sold and he has made an arrangement with a man in the neighborhood to work for him by the day and be paid in produce. This relieves him of some of the responsibility about the perishable things. The Shakers show a most loving disposition towards us, have offered us 2 hundred trees [at] lower [price] than to anyone else on account of our temperance habits, and because we consider fruit a necessary of life, and also wish to come over and help in setting them out. They seem most lovingly drawn towards us. I have done up a little parcel for [her brother] Charles and a copy of Pestalozzi's letters for Mrs. Adams. They should be a study for every Mother. I have written Charles a hasty note but now my mind is too much oppressed to do any thing long which is not connected with the condition of things here. I wish you would explain to him more fully how I am situated, with a large, but fluctuating family, feeble husband, and not wholly persuaded in my own mind that all that *is,* is *best*.

I ought not to write to any body. I told Mr. Thayer on parting with him he must come ten years hence for my opinion about Fruitlands. "Dear Lady," said he, "You will not be here to answer me." Perhaps not; in that case it will speak for itself. It will be a barren wilderness or a fruitful Paradise, I fear, despite of me. My

---

*Probably her niece Elizabeth Willis Wells, then in her early twenties.

Genius is too rigidly set in the old mould to make great progress. I abhor Society as it is, with its fallacies and shams, but I can only be real myself. My neighbor must decide in spite of me or my reproof. I can't live *his* principle.★

I thank you, dear Sam, for your offer to come up. You could do us no particular good, and I know that we could not make you comfortable. I shall shut up Mr. A[lcott] from all care and company. Should he fail again, or anything more acute take place, I shall make known to him, send for Emerson, and consult with him. He has good sense enough not to be afraid of human aids for human ends.

If it will not trouble you too much and you have a direct opportunity to send to Boston, I wish you would get me a good large bottle of Camphor. . . . When he was fainting from exhaustion every few hours last week, I did not even have a tablespoonful of vinegar. I used water freely, but . . . it is almost an essential of life to the nurse if not to the patient to have an odour of camphor or vinegar. . . .

Journal entry

August 26. . . . Visited the Shakers. I saw but little of their domestic or internal arrangements, [but] there is servitude somewhere, I have no doubt. There is a fat, sleek, comfortable look about the men and among the women there is a stiff, awkward, reserve that belongs to neither sublime resignation [n]or divine hope.

Wherever I turn I see the yoke on woman in some form or other. On some it sits easy for they are but hearts of burden. On others pride hushes them to silence; no complaint is made for they scorn pity or sympathy. On some it galls and chafes. They feel assured by every instinct of their nature that they were designed for a higher, nobler calling than to "drag life's lengthening chain along."

★The page is torn at the word "decide."

A woman may perform the most disinterested duties. She may "die daily" in the cause of truth and righteousness. She lives neglected, dies forgotten. But a man, who never performed in his whole life one self-denying act, but who has accidental gifts of Genius, is celebrated by his contemporaries, while his name and his works live on, from age to age.

He is crowned with Laurel while scarce a "stone may tell where *she* lies." Miss Page made a good remark and true as good; that a

Wherever I turn I see the yoke on woman in some form or other.

woman may live a whole life of sacrifice and at her death meekly says I die a *woman*. A man passes a few years in experiments on self denial and simple life and he says, "behold a God." There certainly is more true humility in *woman,* more substantial goodness than in man. Woman lives her thought, man speculates about it. Woman's love is enduring, changeless. Man is fitful in his attachments; his love is *convenient,* not of necessity. Woman is happy in her plain lawn. Man is better content in the royal purple.

Many visitors the last few weeks . . . Mr. Alcott continues feeble. The children all well and deport themselves with more than usual discretion and quietude. . . .

To her brother Charles from Fruitlands in autumn

I am not dead yet, either to life or love. . . . This is a Hotel where man and beast are entertained without pay, and at great expense. I keep saying, 'Oh when will rest come?' I am too generous to tackle anybody [else] into this harrow, for drag as you will you cannot get the ground smooth: the asperities are too sharp, the sinuosities too deep. . . .

It is absurd to suppose that all move in the same circle. . . . [I wish to] permit each to be good in his own way. I do not wish to transcend humanity; I wish to transcend nothing but evil and sin. I hope not to transcend my senses; they are the sentinels to guard the citadel of my soul.

Even our passions are heralds announcing a deep nature. A passionless person is to me a tame, half-whole animal. . . . If rightly governed, [passions] render us invulnerable to All the heresy of Sin.

To Samuel Joseph from Fruitlands

Saturday Morn [November 4, 1843]

Mr. Wyman has given me 5 minutes to say a thousand things in. It is concluded I *believe* that we are to stay here this winter. I will predict nothing but try to fortify myself for all the storms and be grateful for all the healing gales which may be breathed upon me. William [Lane] has been sick a fort night, and Louisa with a dreadful cough, pain in her side and head-ache. Mr. Lane looks miserably and *acts worse*.

The accounts from Miss [Hannah] Robie are quite discouraging. This will be a sad chapter in my book of fate if she too in the absence of Mother and Sisters shall go hence to be no more seen. She has been to me a loving and judicious counselor. . . . We now talk of selling back to Mr. Wyman 30 acres of land on which the house and Barn stand, paying him out of it all the balance now due, and building a cottage on the intervale, planting their Orchard and having a garden. How far this will be enacted the [illegible] saith not.

At present we are loading up wood and apples as the one thing needful. My children and we all are comfortably fixed for clothing, and come what may I shall try that the peace of these dear children be no more disturbed by discussions and doubts. I and they *will* have comfort, a good fire, cheerful faces, and pleasant books. Mr. Alcott walked from Boston in 8 hours on Thursday, seems calm, cheerful, active. I only want to see Mr. Lane in a better mood. It is sad to see greatness so subject to contemptible, pitiable, weakness. But no man is great to his valet, says Sterne or somebody else. Neither is he always sublime to his *house maid.*

Yrs in love and gratitude, Abba

In November, six months after Lane bought the farm, the first mortgage payment came due. Bronson and Lane had no money; Lane had spent all he had on the down payment, and Bronson accumulated only debts. After discussing the matter with Abigail, no doubt, Samuel Joseph declined to pay the seventy-five dollars they owed, causing the farm to go into foreclosure.

To Samuel Joseph regarding the foreclosure

November 11, 1843

Dear S.,

Your letter was duly received and pleased me better than it did the other proprietors of the Estate [Lane and Bronson]. I do not wish you to put a cent *here.* I am sifting everything to its bottom, for I will know the foundation, center and circumference.

They have had an offer for 30 acres by a young farmer in Boxboro, who will give them 25 doll[ar]s an acre, and another offer from Mr. Parker's son who will give them 1400 for the whole. Mr. Lane thought of accepting it, and letting us go out naked. I am ready for it, and should feel it a clean transaction to go with my skin. I do not like the concern. There is a griping propensity somewhere. Mr. Alcott talks of buying the frame of Mr. Wyman's small barn, hauling it to the woods, and building a house, selling part of the land, etc. etc.

A woman may live a whole life of sacrifice and at her death meekly says I die a woman. A man passes a few years in experiments on self denial and simple life and he says, "behold a God."

But I see no clear healthy safe course here in connexion with Mr. L[ane]. It is not clear to me. I am glad you are coming to hear all the pro's and con's. I believe they are satisfied that last summer was worse than lost. People have been [here] and devoured our substance and turned round to scoff at our efforts. Well, never mind me, [I'm] set up for a month; strange if nobody dared to fire and nobody to hit. We'll work out something before Spring. Anna is on her way to Boston to pass a few weeks with Cousin Louisa Willis who is still in her room.

Domestic life is a problem not easily solved.

> In haste, Love to Lu, A.A.

Journal entries

November 20, 1843. Visited Boston. Found myself quite lame which prevented seeing many friends. Home always seems more and more interesting to me after a short absence. Domestic life is a problem not easily solved.

November 29, 1843.* Dear Louey, Your handwriting improves very fast. Take pains and do not be in a hurry. I like to have you make observations about our conversations and your own thoughts. It helps you to express them and to understand your little self.

Remember, dear girl, that a diary should be an epitome of your life. May it be a record of pure thought and good actions, then you will indeed be the precious child of your loving mother.

---

*Louisa May Alcott's eleventh birthday. Abigail recorded in her journal a birthday note she gave her daughter.

December 25, 1843. Christmas. Interchanged little gifts with the children, had a little merry-making in the evening with the neighbor's children. Weather severe, constant succession of snow-storms. My eyes have become quite troublesome. I have humored the weakness by not using them much of evenings. Play with the children, sing and try to cheer the scene within to render the cheer-lessness without more tolerable. We are completely blocked up [by snow]; our neighbor Lovejoy has twice broken a path for us, so that we are able to get the mail.

January 16, 1844. [I] Removed this week from "Fruitlands" to our neighbour Lovejoy's, taking 3 rooms and use of kitchen for 50 cents per week. We find ourselves quite comfortable for winter quarters. Received this week from brother S.J.M. 10 dollars, also Mrs. Whiting paid me 12 for cloak, and cousin M.D.M. sent 10 for silver slice, which I regretted parting with, as it was a gift from my dear Miss Robie, but several calls for money without any visible means to answer them impelled me to part with it. I am sure she would not think hardly of me for it. I have been driven to many of these straits during these last few years but I hope we shall be settled soon to some mode of life which shall either be more independent of the aid of others or less irksome to ourselves.

Mr. Alcott cannot bring himself to work for gain, but we have not yet learned to live without money or means.

March 22, 1844. My friends write very decidedly that it is best not to purchase [a house] but live for the present. Mr. Alcott is dis-satisfied with the whole property arrangement, and has started to-day in hopes of finding a new home established on true and more elevated relations.

It has been a day of soul-sickness to me. I scarcely know where to begin to bring about a more joyous condition, and yet it is wrong to indulge whilst my children are in no wise participa-tors of my anxiety neither can they alleviate my suffering by their sympathy.

In early January 1844 Abigail left Fruitlands with her four daughters to live in three rented rooms on a neighboring farm. Lane took his son to join the Shakers, and some time later Bronson followed Abigail. Details of her thoughts and movements are scarce for this period of marital distress because many letters Abigail wrote were simply cut from the family's bound volume of her correspondence, presumably by Bronson or other family members. Scores of pages of her journals from this period were similarly cut out.

To Samuel Joseph

Harvard, [Massachusetts,] April 9, [18]44

After many deliberations and divers plans to meet the needs of this family, the expectations of our friends, and the wishes of my own heart, we have decided on a plan which came most unexpectedly and opportunely. I had tried in vain here and at Concord for a tenement suitable for us, . . . I have made a proposition which Mr. and Mrs. Lovejoy have acceded to. And the [Lovejoys'] mother agrees too.★ I have taken for 6 months or one year half the[ir] house at Still River which the mother was to occupy, and which by cutting a door into the wood house and one into an adjoining chamber brought my family into quite a distinct range of rooms for them. He charges me $25 doll[ar]s a year for the five rooms, 10 dollars for a garden about ¾ of an acre, he ploughing and setting it ready for the planting, etc. I have suggested cutting a door between our chambers and opening a passageway to the north side of the wood house and which give us access to all the necessary departments without having to pass through their kitchen; also fixing up a little bathing room. He thinks the whole may cost something like 5 or 6 doll[ar]s which I told him I would pay for, as it is for our especial benefit. I

★The Lovejoys were her landlords, to whom she initially paid two dollars a month for three rooms and the use of their kitchen.

hope these arrangements will not be considered extravagant. I know not where we can get quarters for a less[er] sum, without it is in the almshouse, which I am preparing for as fast as possible, that we need not be perplexed ourselves about ways and means, or vex our friends with the to and fro conditions of our life. Our social privileges here are small, educational advantages for my children nothing, but we can live free from debt though it will be much after the fashion as described from "hand to mouth." Mr. A[lcott] has seemed better since his return, though far from well now.

My year's rent begins the 15th. We shall move in a few days. Are either of the Louisas mothers yet?★ Mr. A passed through Boston but heard not a word. Went 3 days with Mr. Emerson. Has been to day to see Mr. Lane at the Shakers. Mr. L[ane] and boy have joined them.

Love to Lucretia and the children. Believe me yours as ever, gratefully and affectionately, A.A.

To Samuel Joseph

Harvard, June 5, [18]44

Dear S,

I received duly per baggage wagon 1 barrel flour, ½ butter, sugar and rice, all very nice and in good order, and for which we are greatly obliged. Our garden looks beautifully, tho' the frost thinned out our beans. June paints a sweet picture from the chamber window. It is just a year since we came to Harvard. It has been a most eventful year to me, or rather I ought to say, a most *significant* one, for it has on the whole been less filled with events than *signs*. . . .

★The two Louisas were Louisa Windship Willis and another married niece.

Have you seen Mrs. Child's letters in the *Courier*?★ Have you got any of them? Those on Old Bull are inimitable. I hope they will be collected into a volume like the others, from New York. Why, my dear S[am], they are the Holy Scriptures to my soul, full of the infinite. . . . The American public do not appreciate her greatness. . . .

By 1839 Abigail's brother Samuel Joseph had completely alienated most of his South Scituate congregation by integrating the seating of his black and white parishioners. Again he left the ministry, now to work for Horace Mann as superintendent of the Lexington Normal School. His family lived in Lexington, only a few miles from the Alcotts. But in 1844, after disagreements with Mann over abolition, Samuel Joseph resigned.

To Samuel Joseph on his resignation from the Lexington Normal School

August 11, [18]44

Dear S[am],

I received your letter announcing your resignation. You held a useful position but you can stand in no useless place anywhere, for you make the place. Place can do little for you, with all your tendencies to do good and communicate. May Providence guide you to the best decisions, and sustain you in all your efforts.

I have been reading with great delight James Martineau's Sermons. Those on the "Kingdom of God within us" are full of salient power and elevated thought. . . . "Many a purpose fit only for ourselves, suited to the peculiarities of our own character and condi-

---

★Lydia Maria Child, the author and abolitionist, was writing letters from New York to the *Boston Courier*.

tions, we must take up in private and in silence pile up effort, after effort, till it be accomplished!" . . .

To Samuel Joseph on the birth of his fourth child

Still River, Sept[ember] 23, [18]44★

Dear S[am],

Your last interesting fact surprised me indeed.† I am truly grateful that our dear L[ucretia] is thus far comfortably through now for nourishment and baby. Assure Lucretia that a drink but of pure cold water will make giving wholesome milk. A pint of slops will neither nourish mother or child. A roast potato or apple (baked sweet apples are best) with a little cream, and *coarse* bread will fatten mother and child. I defy cholic and *nurse* both. Her baby will sleep without paregoric and Mother will eat without dyspepsia. Some most interesting facts have come within my knowledge within the last 2 years.

How do Charlotte and the boys like the little stranger?‡ Assure dear L[ucretia] these are the little angels sent with messages of love if we will only listen and feel their truth. . . .

Tell L[ucretia], when God puts the babies in our laps, he places all the needfuls in its vicinity for its life and health—air, water, and Mother's *titty* is all it wants for a good while.

Around this time her brother Samuel Joseph and his family moved to Syracuse, New York, where he became the minister of the Church of the Mes-

---

★They now rented a house in Still River, a hamlet near Harvard, Massachusetts.

†Lucretia, in her early forties, had given birth to a fourth son, "Bonnie" George May.

‡Lucretia and Samuel Joseph's older children, Joseph, Charlotte, and John Edward May, were fourteen, eleven, and eight, respectively.

siah. In addition to preaching and working for abolition, he became the first
minister in the nation to advocate women's rights from his pulpit.

To Samuel Joseph

Still River, October 6, [18]44

Dear S[am],

Mr. Alcott returned last evening where he has been spending a
week with Mr. Emerson, who intends to help him to the amount
of 500 doll[ar]s to getting a house and suitable garden spot for us.
Our present plan is to move to Concord next Monday into half
of Edmund Hosmer's house; this places us near the scene of our
future home and gives Mr. E[merson] and A[lcott] time to select
and concert means and measure before spring. I do not object to
the plan in as much as it will throw Mr. A more into the society of
those he likes, and may help to mature a wiser and broader scheme
of action than can be concocted in Mr. Alcott's abstractions or
closest cogitations. Emerson will keep a rational view in sight and
there will be less of Ultraism and yet perfect freedom of action. I
dread his falling into that solitary life he led last winter. He is in fine
health and spirits as we are all of us, and I hope you will come and
see us soon. It is on the road from Emerson's south about ½ mile;
stop there and he will direct you. . . . I think Mr. Emerson is very
desirous he [Bronson] come to C[oncord] and I will not oppose
it. Anna and Mr. T talk of opening a school there in the spring.*
Geo[rge] Bradford is teaching there. I can get some kind of work
from the city and can pass very quickly and quietly by the rail-road,
and I know I have only to make the application to get it, if my little
income does not meet the wants of the family. . . . I may have to get
a small cooking stove without I can hire one for the winter as the

_____

*Anna Whiting; Mr. T is unknown.

room I aim to cook in has no fire place. But I think I can manage all at C[oncord] without much cost. But moving about consumes time, life, and money. I am tired of it. But the great idea will be realized before a thousand years I hope, and we shall all be transfixed in eternal marble.★ Give my love to Charlotte and Jos[eph]. And believe yrs affectionately, Abba Alcott

To Samuel Joseph

Concord, December 13 [18]44

Dear S[am],

I am sitting at Mrs. Brook's centre-table to urge upon you the importance of striking with iron while it is hot here.† Mrs. B[rook] as well as myself are just at this among red hot abolitionists. We feel that soon there be no freedom for white or colored man this side [of] Mason and Dixon's line. Mr. Hoar's rebuff has set them all to feeling about for their rights and liberties, and the stiffest conjunctive is almost ready to acknowledge that he has known, the struggle after it convinces them they are in bondage for the fetter of all. If you get this in time do come up on Sunday even[ing]. You will have a room, and you can send a return answer. . . . Mr. A[lcott] is rather desponding for something to do. His chopping wood fixes him up for a day or two, but the spirit yearns for a higher, freer sphere [in which] to act.

Yrs, Abba

★Abigail later added in pencil, "Good."

†The previous month, Judge Samuel Hoar of Salem had been sent by the Massachusetts governor and legislature on a mission to ensure the safety of free black sailors on cotton ships landing in Charleston, South Carolina. Southern politicians attacked and threatened him for "meddling" in their affairs, and he and his daughter Elizabeth had to leave Charlestown under cover. Hoar's reporting of this incident served to further the abolitionist cause.

Journal entries

March 16, 1845. This poetical effort [by Louisa] was quite impromptu, and I think with some success.* Louisa continues to write, has copied all her little verses into a book. She is making great effort to obtain self possession and repose, less excitable and anxious.

March 17. S[amuel] J[oseph] has decided on going to Syracuse.† It makes me a little sad when I try to realize the event. If it casts no shade over the future to me, it surely throws less sunshine over my prospects. But it is well ordered that we should be gently and gradually loosened from those ties to the past which may impede the onward movement. I have lost much in early dear friends but I have gained more independence in myself. I have lost dear friends! But I have gained a dear God, less dependence on earth, more trust in heaven.

Received of S.J. May 10 doll[ar]s; this is from my estate in the hand of S.E. Sewall.

April 1, 1845. Remove from Mr. Hosmer's to my own house, where I hope by leading a quiet, busy life to secure peace to my family and just relations to the world. . . .‡ Life is a medley of care, hope, hate, dissatisfaction, dissipation, trial and appeal. It will be no slight task to ravel our threads of those which have become woven into my own web of life. If I cannot do this I will destroy the whole fabric and begin again on a different scheme.

————

*Louisa, age twelve, had written a poem, which Abigail copied into her journal.

†Samuel Joseph May preached at the Church of the Messiah in Syracuse, where he and most of his family would spend the rest of their lives.

‡The Alcotts rented from the Hosmers before moving into the Concord house they had recently purchased, which they called Hillside. It is now a National Parks site known as Wayside, the name that the Hawthornes, who later bought it from Abigail, gave it.

To Samuel Joseph

Concord, April 17, 1845

My dear brother, It is a long time since we interchanged a line. We ought at least once a month to reassure each other of our life and love. A few days since a gentleman drove up the door and made a call to enquire after you. It was the Baptist clergyman of Lexington. He has just moved to Concord, having made a small gathering of scattered sheep into his fold here. I fear they are mostly goats, if he does not fleece them they will turn. His name is Bowers. He spoke most loving[ly] of you and your labours while at Lexington to promote a better condition of things. Also I met a Miss [Merrion] one of the "Ancient Sisters" who eulogized you to the third heaven and could scarce leave you there but must see you fairly resting in Abraham's bosom. . . .

Mr. Alcott has begun upon his garden, giving the children 3 hours instruction and they are doing well. Our prospects of scholars or any other means of living seems to be anything but encouraging. But I hope on; trying to do the best for each day that I can, fearing to doubt the Eternal Providence that for 6000 years has extended such paternal and bountiful care of Mankind and has promised to succor those who put their trust in him.

I have less confidence in force and activity that I used to have. . . . But there is a higher wisdom of the soul, derived from insight which dispenses with it; this I would attain. For if you do not get all by trusting much, yet you learn to do without, which is the nobler life and leads to true independence. This is the discipline I would give my daughters and myself also. I have had enough already to make me feel its worth and security. Nothing makes one so indifferent to the pain and mosquito-thrusts of life as the consciousness of being morally invulnerable. The wound is but skin deep. They may bruise but cannot disease or distress us.

Mr. Alcott leads a solitary life, passing an evening occasionally with Mr. Emerson, and a circle of young people to converse [with]. But his existence is immaterial. The unseen and Eternal is his care and hope. He says the world has scoffed him. His friends betrayed him, and he waits in patience for the hour when intolerance and prejudice shall crucify him.

I have proposed several times to the girls to write to Charlotte, and I think if she would write to them *first* they would like to. Louisa is very free in her expression and happy in her conceptions. I read a few of her little poems to Elizabeth Hoar and she thought them quite good. Two she thought very superior. I encourage [Louisa's] writing; it is a safety valve to her smothered sorrow which might otherwise consume her young and tender heart.

Do give my kindest love to Lucretia and all the children, and snatch a moment to tell me all about them and yourself, Abba

To Samuel Joseph

Concord, June 8, [18]45

Dear S[am],

. . . My girls are doing well. Louisa enjoying the season, weeds with her father like a Trojan. Anna sticks to the books, and Elizabeth is smiling on everything as if love was as cheap as dirt. . . . Your dear [son] John sent by E. your daguerreotype. It is your anxious look, Mr. May the reformer, not the Unitarian minister of early times.

Concord, July 21, [18]45

Dear S[am],

. . . If you have any books, such as Johnson or Pope, or Cowper or Bunyan, any of those standard authors, that I might keep a few years, till the children may need them, I should be grateful. They are authors not much called for just now by the generality of readers, but of which I shall never weary. I love them as old friends; their very bindings have a charm. . . .

I exchanged while there [in Boston] the silver teapot, and the children's baby spoons, no longer of any use to them as spoons, for a half dozen silver forks and fruit knives, having one marked for each of the girls as a gift from their grandfather. I thought this a better form to own them in, more useful now, and easier to do tribute hereafter more equally as we may be called to separate; as we eat apples a good deal the knives are useful because easily kept bright, and not so injurious to the teeth. I thought it a good disposition of my little legacy, more easily divided among my children when on my death.

I should like to know if you think I can spare from my little fund as much as two hundred and 50 dollars. . . . Perhaps Aunt Davenport or Benj[amin] Willis or Mr. Greele or G.B. Emerson would each contribute 5 or 10 dollars [to us].* It would be a trifle for them but everything to me. When I go to Boston and see the lavish waste of money on that which satisfieth not it makes my heart faint. . . . Anna sews exquisitely and Louisa is grateful for any occupation. She is still—†

Concord, August 9, [18]45

My dear S., . . . I wish to say to you sincerely, that I am quite unwilling you should send me any money in Nov.; if you are obliged to *borrow* you have no right to give. You have had an expensive year and your family must be expensive, to exhaust all your income, or you must allow your desire to do good, to perhaps your just capability for doing so. I was grieved to find you were straitened for means. I have been willing to spend my little that I might have more faculties for earning something, and putting the girls in a way

---

*An aunt, two brothers-in-law, and a close family friend.
†The rest of the letter was cut away.

to do something for themselves, without being driven from home for support, and to be spared that most afflictive of all conditions, dependence on relatives. It mars friendships, chills love, destroys confidence. Thank John for his visit. It was very kind of him! . . .

Yrs, A.A.

Journal entry

September 5, 1845. Miss Ford announces her intentions of leaving us before winter, another demonstration of the fact that we, or I, am not ready for associative life or any other great responsibility. . . .* I am glad to be thrown once more on my own efforts to do and be to my daughters what I believe I am capable of being, and I shall put myself in closer more intimate communication with them than ever . . . but I am not sure that a mother should ever yield so great a trust to another; my children will not bear to be put from me. They have always felt an unfaltering trust in their mother and if she had greatly betrayed it, I think it could not have been so merrily sustained. I shall rally all my power, shake off all extraneous influence, and depend on my own moral and intellectual might. *Deo volente* I shall not be defeated.

Miss Ford's perceptions are right; I ought not to take other people's children when my own are such faulty specimens of parental impotence. But her conclusions are never-the-less not all correct. She thinks me desultory, and the children indolent. A woman who has never known the maternal relation can know but little of the resources of a mother's love to bring about most important and desirable results. . . .

---

*Sophia Ford had boarded with the Alcotts at Hillside and helped with housework and teaching the children.

Journal fragment, c. 1845

Wisdom and love, celestial pair,
in matrimonial union are.
If wisdom vex, and love contend,
domestic bliss is at an end.

To Samuel Joseph

Concord, September 19, [18]45

My dear brother,

. . . Mr. Alcott has been gone 4 days, having been sent for to attend Junius, whom they found in an alarming condition, taken start raving crazy, without any previous symptoms of indisposition of any kind.* He had wished much to see Amos [Bronson] for several weeks. They therefore sent for him, thinking the effect might be favorable. We have heard nothing yet. . . .

Louisa is in fine health and spirits, has gained great repose and health this summer. Miss Ford's influence has been very favorable on her. . . .

Affectionately, Abba.

Abigail attended a talk by the social reformer Robert Owen, who had founded a cooperative community at New Harmony, Indiana.

Concord, December [18]45

My Dear Brother,

. . . Mr. Owen is the most hopeful person I ever met, feeling quite sure that he should see a radical change while he lives.

---

*Seven years later Junius Alcott committed suicide by throwing himself into a threshing machine.

I admire his enthusiasm . . . and his project for rebasing, recon-structing, and reforming society so that a new and harmonious whole shall be found in a few years. One thing is certain that if he cannot reorganize the social compact, he certainly has discovered and analyzed the 5 Great Evils from which society is suffering, and which are working out the Great Disharmony, disorganization and ruin: "Religious Perplexities, Disappointment of the Affections, Pecuniary Difficulties, Intemperance, Anxiety for the welfare of Offspring." These he says are the foundation of all the present sin, sorrow, and defeat. *I believe it; I know it* at least from my own experi-ence from 4 of these evils, growing out of the present arrangements of society—wholly arbitrary, totally conventional. And I can trace the destitution and misery to hundreds within my observation pro-ceeding from the same causes.*

We have had a nice visit from Charles and wife; she is a reserved, but I think self-possessed, woman.†

I see by the papers that you are striking heavy blows at the "Texas rivetings" before that chain [of another slave state] is indissolubly fastened upon us.‡ It is a long one found of innumerable links. I have lost all my faith in the means now using; for the half is not told. Annihilate slave produce, [then] free labor will be in demand and North as well as South will *feel* the expediency if not see the *righteousness* of *free* service to hard labor. Strike a blow at cotton fac-tories and you touch the main spring to their trap! But who is suf-ficient for these things? We must all work in our own way doing the best we can ourselves, and hoping the most for others.

My girls are going to the District School. . . .

Yrs, Abba

---

*Later, in 1876, Abigail added, "Very good."
†Charles May married late, had four children, and died, in 1856, at sixty-eight.
‡The annexation of Texas as the thirty-eighth state in the union raised the issue of a new slave state, which Samuel Joseph and other abolitionists opposed.

Concord, Feb[ruar]y 15, [18]46.

My dear brother, I received your letter containing a draught on Wells Wetherbee Co. which was cashed at the Concord Bank $20.00 doll[ar]s. This will complete all my payments and leaves me a balance of 7.00. I have been dreadfully perplexed. But it has taught me a good lesson, not to rely on the good *intentions* of my friends. It is a shiftless kind of life, but I do not see my way through yet. My hope is in a school, and Mr. Alcott's thrift in the management of his land. The girls are getting on well with their studies. But I don't much relish their being absent 6 hours. . . .

Now for my own part I had rather have the clownish, rough, good surge of uneducated people, than so much of the seeming which is apt to be the weakness of more refined society. If a man don't use good grammar, "he's a man for ain't that" and love him for his manhood. That word "Good Society" is a bubble. Society as it is now constructed is a false compact [of] cunning, competition, force and fraud. . . . *seeming*, not *being* is the order of the day. We all understand it, and all consent, either tacitly or actively, to the *appearance* rather than the *fact*.

I feel so comfortable now I am out of debt that I can afford to advance a little heresy. The world vexes me, and when I am rid of it I like to turn and rend. You'll think this very Christlike, and loving. Remember me affectionately to Lucretia and the dear children . . .

Concord July, [18]46.

My dear S[am], On reaching home after an absence of a few days I found your letter. The check for $25 was cashed at the Bank but not as a Bank transaction. The president took it to Boston for 50 c[en]ts discount. I am truly grateful for the money. I have not had a penny since you sent the last until I went to Boston. S.E.S. loaned me $20 saying he was still in advance of my income. The place [Hillside house] is looking beautifully and promises to realize all our expectation if we can be sustained upon it a little longer. As yet it is but little in the way of a living. But industry always is rewarded in some manner, and we are a laboring industrious family. George Bond presented Anna with a German Dictionary and other aids occur for our children which encourage me to hope all will be well in the end. It is disagreeable to have to make an advertisement of one's condition every few months as "wanting" but it is worse and more fatal to the purity and progress of the soul to be compelled to daily put oneself in communication with false, unrighteous principles. It is safer to *have* less, to *do* less, to *be* less of the world than to be of it and lose the beauty and truthfulness of our being. I see so many corruptions, delusions, abomination in society. . . . Truth never is *popular*. The same spirit that mobs your peace sentiments cuts down Mr. Frost's trees, and jeers Mrs. Alcott because she expects the young men to beware of the fascination, the glitter, and the glare of military parade.

> *It is safer to have less, to do less, to be less of the world than to be of it and lose the beauty and truthfulness of our being.*

Oh, dear Sam, we want the Poem but we must have the Protest too. Declare the truth tho' it bring the condemnation of the whole world on your head. . . . It is for love and duty to bear and forbear with heroic endurance the evils of our day, the sins of our generation. Freed not like my sister "Abigails" to go upon the housetops or among the milk trucks to declare the besetting evils of the day, but I can sit on my hearthstone with this band of tender virgin maidens and testify by a simple life and quiet forbearance against the sins of dress, self-indulgence and all the petty corruption as well as the grosser evils which beset society.*

Oh Sam, dedicate yourself to Peace, keep your pulpit if it is only to secure a place from which to declare and testify this truth. It is the cornerstone of the true church. Our nation in its principles is

*Abigail added in 1876, "True and good."

becoming corrupt and abusive, warlike, and degraded. It will cut off its own head with its own weaknesses. But faith in the power of forbearance will remove mountains of hindrance or by love and endurance transmute
rocks to feather beds on which to repose in
sweet security.

Truth never is popular.

It was a great day in Dedham. We all went, in company with the Emersons, Mrs. Brooks, and a large delegation from—*

Love to all, Abba Alcott

November 2, [18]46

Dear Brother,

. . . We have lately introduced a new member to our family circle. What the effect will be is doubtful. The compensation is a temptation to make the experiment, and if she does not prove too great an annoyance shall keep her a year. It is a daughter of William Stearns's who has been for the last 5 years becoming more and more confused, until they cannot manage her at home. He brought her from Nova Scotia intending to place her at an asylum for the Insane but Dr Jackson and Jarvis advised a private family. Miss Robie urged me to try her one month. This I did faithfully and I found nothing in the girl now 15 years old but what with Mr. A[lcott]'s gentle persevering discipline I could manage, have engaged the care of her for one year, for 4 doll[ar]s per week. Mr. Stearns said he expected to pay at least 200 a year, and is preparing to return home, apparently much pleased at our arrangements. She is in a state of sad mental imbecility, the result I should think of mismanagement in early life. She reminds me continually of Caroline Stearns, odd, imperious, imbecile. I shall give the girls the use of the school-room all winter, for Elizabeth [Stearns] asks innumerable questions and must have a patient answer. She is a totally irresponsible being, and like a young

*The page is torn off at this point.

child must be gradually developed into love, usefulness and happiness. I shall have less time for reading and other pursuits which I love with my girls but if by faithful care of this bewildered child we can make her path more . . . straight I shall be well repaid for the sacrifice of personal comfort. I know of no so righteous way of adding to our income and paying our debts. I have been to Salem with Miss Robie. . . .

Journal entry

November 29, 1846. Mr. Alcott's and Louisa's birthday. . . . I gave Mr A ½ ream of paper and Louisa an ornamented pen-stock. . . . I will copy on the opposite page a few lines accompanying Louisa's pen; it was not a fruitless attempt.

> *Oh! May this pen your muse inspire*
> *when wrapt in pure poetic fire,*
> *To write some sweet, some thrilling verse*
> *a song of Love, or Sorrow's lay,*
> *or Duty's clear but tedious way.*
> *In brighter hope rehearse.*
> *Oh let your strain be soft and high*
> *of crosses here, of crowns beyond the sky.*
> *Love guide your pen, inspire your theme*
> *And from each note a gush of gladness stream.*

Note to Louisa with the birthday gift

Dearest, accept from your mother this pen and for her sake as well as your own use it freely and worthily. Let each day of this your 15th year* testify to some good word or work; and let your diary receive a record of the same. I know there will be born with your spirit, new hopes, new gifts for God is near to help the trusting loving heart. Lift up your soul then to meet the highest for that alone can satisfy your great yearning nature. Your temperament is a peculiar one, and there are few or none who can intelligently help you. Set about the work of formation of character, reformation of habits, and believe me you are capable of ranking among the best, and attain for yourself a sweet peace when you are called hence. Industry, patience, love creates, endures, gives all things, these are attributes of the almighty, and they make us mighty in all things. I wish you a happy birth-day, may eternal love sustain you, infinite wisdom guide you, may the sweetest peace reward you.

Conscious of Louisa's quick mind and deep thoughts and the brevity of her formal education, Abigail often encouraged her daughter to write.

To Louisa

[undated, possibly 1846]

I am sure your life has many fine passages well worth recording, and to me they are very precious. Do write a little each day, dear, if but a line, to show me how bravely you begin the battle, how patiently you wait for the rewards sure to come when the victory is nobly won.

---

*On her fourteenth birthday, Louisa was entering her fifteenth year of life.

To Samuel Joseph

Concord December 4, [18]46

Dear S[am],

. . . I have just heard that Louisa has a son, names him Joseph May.* How thoughtlessly this domestic martyrdom is encircled in married life! What a volume might be written on the Heroines of private life! There is a courage of endurance, as high as that of action. There are martyrs who wear no crowns, and for whom no faggots burn; those who are so accustomed to sacrifice 'self' and to die daily that their lives are surrounded by a halo of glory. . . .

Mr. Garrison reports himself home again, alive and well. I hope he will have magnanimity enough to record, not with black lines, but with a chastened spirit and becoming decency, the death of poor Rogers.† His party have done him bad service in so grossly defending a human man at the expense of so much divine principle. Garrison loves power. . . . Alas! When will men love mercy better than sacrifice!

> *What a volume might be written on the Heroines of private life!*

Elizabeth Willis I hear is coming to pass Christmas with Louisa Willis. We are all well. E[liza] S[tearns] is a great care, but there is some satisfaction for there is a change for the better.‡ In haste with dearest love to all, Aunt Abba. Write soon.

---

*Louisa Willis Wells, Abigail's niece.

†Nathaniel Peabody Rogers, founder of an abolitionist paper in New Hampshire, was at his death, in 1846, estranged from Garrison.

‡Eliza Stearns was a mentally disabled teenager for whom Abigail had agreed to care.

Journal entries

December 1846. This month has been full of interest. Preparations for the "Christmas tree." The birth of a daughter to Charles, on Christmas day. The arrival of a [fugitive] slave named for the present John, an inmate in my family until some place where work can be provided. An amiable, intelligent man just 7 weeks from the "House of Bondage."

December 31. Most beautiful dawn, as mild as May. Horizon brilliant, calm, translucent . . . I rose early to give John his breakfast that he might go to his work by early dawn. I was repaid for my efforts by meeting God; the interview was short, but *real*.

In looking over my accounts for the year 1846, I find we have recieved [*sic*] from friends and our own produce 478, and find we are owing 254. These arrearages are very distressing because I feel so helpless. Where to curtail, or how to produce is alike impracticable to me. My children are at no schools, I never rode [a coach] to the amount of one dollar since I lived in Concord, excepting to Boston where I have been called to go on business, I purchase no articles of dress excepting cotten [*sic*], calico and shoes. Although much that I receive is useless finery or uncomfortable articles of wearing apparel, yet we go without many things which we really need as common comforts. Our food is simple, our recreations not expensive, and yet I am constantly finding myself involved or perplexed for the want of money.

My friends are wearied with my applications for help, and it does not seem to occur to them that each putting a fraction at interest for me, would relieve all this distressing embarrassment and give us a comfort which we deserve at their hands. I shall ask no more [of them] but help at the work of life while there is work to do, intelligently, conscientiously, as fast and far as I can. . . .

To Samuel Joseph

Concord, January 13, 1847

My dear Brother,

Your two admirable sermons have compensated for the long interval of exchanged letters. But one sometimes feels a longing for a little individualism. I am so used up these short days, and my eyes are good for nothing in the evening, that I can scarce find a moment for the compliments of the season. . . .

We have had an interesting fugitive [slave] here for 2 weeks, right from Maryland. He was anxious to get to Canada and we have forwarded him the best way we could. His sufferings have been great, his intrepidity unparalleled. He agrees with us about Slave Produce; he says it is the only way the abolition of the slave can ever be effected. He says it will never be done by insurrection. There are never enough [slaves] agreed in one mind to make it possible, and then the fears of the women overcome the resolution of the men and keep them back, and the slaves are treacherous and betray each other. . . .

We are feeling all about here the terrors of war. Our neighbor Hosmer's 2nd son, a fine lad, enlisted and has been carried to the insane asylum bewildered on the subject of his duty to his country and his duty to his family. . . . The misery among the Irish is dreadful, husbands, sons, brothers. The regiment is principally made up of foreigners. We are using up these poor fellows as the monkey did the cat's paw to get the chestnuts out of the pot. We shall use their paws and then eat the nuts, giving them the shells. Ah me! How true, man's inhumanity to man*—

---

*The remainder of this letter is cut out of the bound volume.

Employment

Having finally recognized that Bronson would not support them, Abigail began looking for a job. Despite her paid boarders and sewing and the contributions of her elder daughters, she could not accumulate enough to maintain Hillside, which needed repairs. Although her society expected a married woman not to work outside the home, Abigail took financial matters into her own hands. She could sell her house, she thought, and earn an income. How she would accomplish the latter was an open question. Around this time the Emersons recommended that she consider taking a job as matron of a Maine water-cure establishment, the nineteenth-century equivalent of a health spa.

To Samuel Joseph

Concord, Sept[ember] 12, 1847

To Sam,

. . . Concord has been one great hospital for the past month, sickness and death all about us. . . . I helped to convey to the city a sweet baby of 2 years who revived just long enough to recognize its luxurious nursery at Mrs. Bancroft's mansion in Winthrop Place. We thought for an hour it would be charmed back into life, but the little spirit was already too weary of the baubles which this world had to bestow and closed its weary eyes to open them where realities alone can satisfy. . . . I think had I seen the child in its first symptoms I would have saved its life, its mother's grief, its father's debt of $50. This seems presumption because I have had no education or diploma, but common sense, common honesty, and the Mother wit of an old woman often accomplishes what counsels and prescriptions fail to do. . . .

I am expecting to visit Waterford [Maine], 40 miles below Portland, have been invited to take the matronage of the water cure if they can secure to me $50 doll[ar]s per annum, shall accept, hire a small tenement in the neighborhood for the family and feel my way out of this $200 doll[ar] debt as fast as possible. We have neither money [n]or credit here, and the girls are wretched about our predicament. More of this anon. Food, rent, clothing are cheap there, [there are] 80 patients, good pay, my labor not so hard as at home, although my responsibilities seem greater.

To Ralph Waldo Emerson

October 4, 1847

For Mr. Emerson, at Theodore Parker's, Bedford House
Mr. Emerson,

Mrs. E[merson] received the enclosed letter for you by this morning's mail, and thought its contents might be of some use to you in your interview with Mr. Parker.★ I am unexpectedly called to the city on business today and avail myself of the privilege to bear to you the pacquet. And oh! our dearest well-beloved friend, may I bear to you also one long earnest grateful remembrance from myself and children for all you are to us, invaluable as an influence and a love, all you are in yourself gracious, generous, good.

★The Rev. Theodore Parker, an influential Unitarian minister, was close to the Mays.

My children rise up and call you blessed, their parents ask the priceless, to love and serve you—

In haste yours ever and forever, Abba Alcott

To Samuel Joseph

Concord, November 23, [18]47

My dear brother, . . . I have just dispatched Anna for Walpole and am looking for a situation for Louisa.★ I hope Elizabeth will go to Miss Robie.† My plans are all undefined. My hopefulness is greater than usual, my helplessness never as apparent. Mr. Alcott is driving at his arbor.‡ I am pulling my house to pieces for the carpenter and painter. . . .

I had a curious speculation on the condition of woman the other day. Told Mr. Alcott I thought there was some mistake when she was created. It was an afterthought, indeed Adam's fancy for a companion first suggested it to Almighty power, and she was called into being after all other animals were made and pronounced *good,* but no such benediction was pronounced on her, but a tacit curse. And she has ever been an illogical, indefinable medley of good and evil, angel and devil, in consequence. I think God is a little ashamed of this piece of his handiwork, and therefore takes little account of us. We owe man a grudge for desiring us, and then caring so little for providing for us.

My love to Lucretia. I know she will not think my speculation without some wit, if little wisdom and no piety. . . .

★Abigail's brother-in-law Benjamin Willis and his family lived in Walpole, New Hampshire. A "situation for Louisa" meant paid work.

†Elizabeth, twelve, would board with Robie at the Sewall's on Beacon Hill.

‡A decorative arbor in Emerson's garden.

I see by the papers Mr. Garrison has been your guest. I hope H. G. Wright will give him some health principles as yet unknown to him. He lives by no law and he will die by consequence.

Feb[ruar]y 8, [18]47

Dear S[am],

All is agreeably arranged except my conscience which is a dreadful ticklish thing on money matters. It does not seem right to use any obligation from you, and it shall be my effort to relieve you all I can. I have taken the ship into my own command, but whether I shall do better as Captain than I have as mate, the revenue and record of the year must decide. At least I think I shall keep better soundings, and ascertain oftener and more correctly whether I am sailing in deep waters or in shallows. We have been nearly wrecked twice. Mr. Alcott thinks we shall never be safe until we get a hut on Walden Pond where with our beans, books, and peace we shall live honestly and independently. But habits are tyrants as well as laws and customs. I do think time, labor well devised, and conscientious simplicity of life will keep us afloat. I had rather sail on this vast ocean of life in a well trimmed ship than anchor myself on the shores of a lake even tho' the smooth bosom of the water reflects the purest heaven. I must think action here is a duty, contemplation is necessary . . . but doing is coextensive with *being*. Indeed I find so many areas of action that it requires great patience and philosophy to look quietly on or only verbally protest. The man is to be paid by the rise on cotton. Here is a case of actual oppression stealing the only article acceptable to the poor for clothing! Shoot the husbands and strip the widows and orphans! I felt as if I wanted to head a pledge to neither buy or wear it. Next comes the Dis-Union question and the Famine claim. One feels a despair when there are so great evils abroad, and so few remedies at home. Too thick throng the evils we cannot obviate, the miseries we cannot relieve.

As Miss [Margaret] Fuller in her admirable letter on London, its luxury and its poverty, says, "I pity the English noble with this difficult problem before him, and such need of a quick solution. Sad is his life if a conscientious man. Sadder if not. To a man of good heart each day brings its purgatory of irremediable ills, which he knows not how to bear, yet to which he fears to become insensible." It is sometimes so on this side the Atlantic. How can we leave undone? Yet what can we safely do? Ah let me rest, after my weary flight, with broken wing over the two hemispheres of misery, and nestle a brief space in my warm, snug house where amid the cheery laugh of these unpledged gangsters I am tempted to acknowledge "where ignorance is bliss 'tis folly to be wise." . . .

Have you seen John Brown's criticism on your Sermon (Rights of Woman). We thought it good. Your [Harvard] classmate Caleb Cushing has received a commmission from Gov. [George] Briggs as commander of the Mass. Regiment of Volunteers. . . . Send me a Syracuse paper occasionally. I like to feel the atmosphere you breathe.

Yrs, AA

To Louisa, age fourteen

Boston, Sun[day] September 29, 1847

Dear Louisa, your tuneful note breathed in my office so softly, so sweetly, has not fallen on a deaf ear, or old heart. But my time has been occupied all day with those little details of life essential to our social position but oh so disruptive to an individual peace and progress. It is these things in our City life which make me long for the country, long for quiet days and simple joys which do not deteriorate the character, but keep it innocent and true. My Diary! Your Diary! only to think that we neither of us snatch a moment to notch our days! Can they be profitably spent if not a moment can be spared to record the fact that we lived? What is time doing to us? Oh, my daughter, if we can make no note of it, shall we only lament its loss? No. No. Occupy, live, learn, love more and more each moment, and record what we know of our self, if we know nothing of another. We are not today what we were yesterday, [n]or can we be tomorrow what we are today. The floodtide of our existence takes us a little farther each day, and the ebb erases the footprints of our yesterday's steps.

I thank you, dear Louisa, for reminding me that I can do anything for you. I am sure when I do anything for my children, I do most for myself, and let us oftener cheer each other with the fact that we love each other. Half a century is nearly told for me. I must post my books to see with what debt and credit I open the new account!

To Anna, age sixteen, teaching in Walpole, New Hampshire★

Concord, December 1847

. . . Simplicity of manners and a well informed mind, with a deep courage, truthful purpose will place you in the best circles. . . . You will derive much aid by the frequent thought that, on the whole, "All things are for the best." You will be sustained by the perusal of books on morals, always reading these in direct reference to your own improvement, rather than amusement.

★Anna was boarding with her Willis and Wells cousins, making money to send home.

To Samuel Joseph

Concord, January 10, 1848

My dear Brother, . . . Aunt Holland has just sent me the sum of $200. This I have divided amongst Mr. Alcott's creditors, and my own, as equally as I could, having a small balance on several accounts. Anna is passing the winter very delightfully with Elizabeth Wells. My E[lizabeth] went to spend the winter with Miss Robie but was so homesick, was obliged to return. . . . We are having charming letters from Mr. Emerson who is having a great time with the British public although there is great diversity of opinion about him.★ We miss him exceedingly; he was our "woodnote" Chanter as well as our Enchanter. Concord is a cold, heartless, Brainless, soulless place. It is very difficult to excite into thought, move into action, or warm into love, this stupid community.

I suppose you see the Liberator. Garrison is again at the helm. They are getting up a subscription to get him a house. Fredrick Holland is made agent of the Unitarian Association; just the man. I think we are rising in the world. I had a beautiful bookmark sent me from the Anti-Slavery fair, words in gold heads with these words and in this manner:

> *Samuel J. May*
> *"Love is the fulfilling of the Lord."*

They were for sale at 25 c[en]ts a piece and every one was gold. I have tried to find out who worked the beautiful [letters] and sent [it] to me, but can neither find the man or the donor.

★Emerson was on a tour of England.

Have you see Charles Sumner's letter about Mr. Palfrey's note?★ We have got one *man* in Congress, and that *one* is an abolitionist. And Oh! Dear Sam, the power of a good man! It is more convincing and persuasive than the logic of a wise one. The school men are less known and remembered than the practical *loving* Jesus, beautiful in his works, irresistible in his words. Even God is more known to us by his goodness and love than by his power or glory. Power and glory are relative terms. Goodness and love are essential characteristics.

Power and glory are relative terms. Goodness and love are essential characteristics.

"Show me thy glory, said the Lord. I will make my goodness pass before thee." "Good works!" says Charles Sumner. "Such even now is the Heavenly Ladder on which angels are ascending and descending, while weary humanity on pillows of stone slumbers heavily at its feet." Have you ever heard his oration before the "literary societies of Amherst College" last August? If you have not, let me send it to you. I have 2 copies. It is beautiful, grand, and pious.

. . . Your Thanksgiving Sermon was excellent. I wish Concord and Boston had such faithful gospel delivered unto them. Many are perishing for the bread of life. Many hunger and know not *for what*. Many are sinful but know not *with* what.

Remember me most affectionately to Lucretia, Charlotte, John, Joseph, and the dear little "Gem," a "Boy who makes dear his father's home."† Goodbye, write soon, that I may know where we stand.

Yrs in haste, Abba Alcott.

---

*Charles Sumner, a U.S. senator from Massachusetts, supported abolishing slavery; John G. Palfrey was a Massachusetts congressman and Sumner's friend.

†The baby of the May family, "Bonnie" George, two years old.

Sunday, February 13, 1848

My Dear Brother,

. . . I hope to sell the place or get Charles to come and join us, stock the place with a cow, horse, cart, and pig, chickens and doves.* Then we can do as other people do, make the land, fruit and milk support us, without this constant appeal to our friends for help, which is more distressing to us, and disastrous to the comfort and independence of our children. . . . I will bake and wash for both families. Mr. A[lcott] and Charles shall divide their labors as they please. . . . Mr. Alcott will yield to any plan of mine. He is so helpless here as things now are. . . . Anna is to continue the school at Walpole. I am at a loss what to do for the other girls; they are needing occupation. They are healthy, active and intelligent. They ought to have some trade, art, or accomplishments with which they could get a support. Mr. Alcott says, "Make no arrangements for them; the place or work will come when they are prepared. Anna no sooner was ready than the niche she could best fill was provided without any effort of ours, a little domestic school." I have given you before a specimen of his faith. . . .

One of Abigail's money-making schemes was for Louisa, fifteen, to learn the art of bronze painting.

Concord, February 29, 1848

. . . I have lately had a very kind offer from Mrs. Reed (Mary-Ann Howell Williams that was) to give Louisa her board [in Boston] for a month and have her take lessons of Mr. Day in bronze painting. His course of 12 lessons is $10 doll[ar]s. Mrs. R says he has never left a pupil till they could prepare the coloring and execute something very handsome by themselves. I think I shall accept for her, and I have no doubt Miss Robie will furnish the $10. She [Louisa]

---

*She envisioned selling Hillside and living with her brother Charles's family.

saw his specimens—landscapes, baskets, boxes, and paper mache articles. This would be a very useful accomplishment because she could furnish articles for the fancy stores in her own room.

[Louisa] will never endure anything like publicity. She must have retirement, agreeable occupation, and protective, provident care about her. She has most decided views of life and duty, and nothing can exceed the strength of her attachments, particularly for her mother. She reads a great deal. Her memory is quite peculiar and remarkably tenacious. I have thought if I could give her an *art*— and Elizabeth the accomplishment of music—and Anna with her acquirements in language—that we might all combine our various gifts and open a school on some new plan. . . .

In the late spring of 1848, at age forty-seven, Abigail moved to inland Maine to become matron of the Waterford water-cure spa. She took with her her youngest daughter, Abby May, and her fifteen-year-old ward, Elizabeth Stearns, leaving Bronson and her daughters Louisa and Elizabeth in Concord.

Boston (at Miss Robie's room), April 16, 1848

Dear S[am],
    . . . I have just returned from Portland [Maine] where I visited our dear [sister] Eliza's tomb, "the last of earth" for her. I never knew before of this beautiful inscription on the monument. . . . I took so much sweeter counsel of memory than I could of consciousness that I lingered around till shades of evening warned me I was a stranger neither knowing or known of the multitude about me. . . . I went to see Mr. Farrar on account of the establishment at Waterford, at which he wished me to preside as matron in case my place was sold. But having just received a declining answer from the man who thought of purchasing [my Concord house], I find I am still tied here. [Concord].

It is curious to see how little others can judge for us. My friends are constantly saying, why don't you do something? Will I accept the first thing that seems at all adapted to my genius? Then they beset me, "Oh, don't leave Concord. Oh, don't sell your place."

There is nothing for us there as things are now conducted. If I am not anxious I cannot be joyous while we are so helpless, so dependent . . .

Journal entries

May 11, 1848. I arrived in Waterford . . . to ascertain . . . its capability to support me and my family. . . . I separate myself for the summer from this dear household of mine, that I may be re-united if possible on more easy and comfortable terms in the fall.

May 16. Little Abba and I are adjusting our room, and arranging the house, bringing something like superficial order out of central chaos. . . . We have great discussions at the table on diet. Dr. Fisher and Mr. Farrar [are] quite desultory in all their habits, and without any fixed law of moral or physical discipline for their being.

How little of ourselves we know. Before a grief the heart has felt! But, the lessons that we learn of woe. . . .

May 18–21. Receiving dear letters from home. They are getting reconciled to my absence. Louisa seems the least well provided for.* Her life is not sufficiently diversified. Anna is doing finely at Walpole, her little school gives her agreeable employment and she sees society at Cousin Elizabeth's which is favorable to the cultivations of her manners. Abba is not well provided for. [I] must not keep her here; it is selfish. The bowling alley and stable are attractive; she sees sights and sounds which are disastrous to the innocence and purity of childhood.

---

*Louisa was now fifteen and Anna, seventeen.

To her family describing her
daily schedule at the spa

I rise at four [a.m.], pack E[liza Stearns] in her wet sheet, then fly through the long passage ways to the baths, get my plunge . . . get back to my room, dress, look on the lake, read or write till five. Go then to the kitchen and get all in order there, then to the breakfast room and see that the glasses are nicely cleaned, the knives in order, etc. To the drawing room next, weep, dust, arrange music books, etc. This takes me till six. I then unpack E[liza] and awake [Abby] May, wash and dress her. Set the two to walking. . . . After breakfast, arrange curtains for patients' rooms, give out bed linens, see that slops are removed and floor wiped up. At 11, give E. a dripping sheet and a wash down, put her to walk, sew or clean as is most pressing. Dine at half past twelve. After dinner, visit the patients' rooms, see that all here are provided with the needfuls. Then talk with Mr. Farrar and Dr. Fisher about the best methods of diet; sew on towelling, bed linen, and . . . give E. a dripping sheet and washdown, at five [p.m.] walk and have supper at six, Dr. Fisher usually giving us some sweet music, or I walk with the children, taking a little ramble, and then to bed.

To Samuel Joseph from the spa

Waterford [Maine], June 14, 1848

My dear brother,

I was very happy to get another demonstration of your remembrance and just now, absent as I am from home and dear familiars, it seemed very precious to have you looking after one of the scattered fragments of the family, once numerous and dear. I have been here about six weeks, . . . at 5 doll[ar]s per week. . . . I have left Mr. Alcott, Louisa and Elizabeth to take care of each other. Anna is passing the summer and has a little school at E[lizabeth] W. Wells's, Walpole.★ My health is admirable and so are all my family in rugged good health and happiness. They are feeling a little tender about my absence, but they will get accustomed to it, and there is more pleasure to me in laboring myself than looking up the precarious pittance which has given us a restless ease, quite depressing and questionable in its best aspect. . . .

But you will have some curiosity to know about my new home. Conceive of Alpine scenery. You have been to the White Mountains. Well, we are on the highway thither. 45 miles below Portland, a most exquisite spot. Lakes all about us, and such mountains. Nothing can be more grand than the reverberations of the thunder among the hills. Our household is now about 17, the cold weather has intimidated the patients and they postpone coming. . . . Dr. M . . . is the consulting physician and comes when sent for. He has skill but no manner, and [is] much of a buffoon.

My labors are arduous but the women are pleasant and I harness in to every heavy job giving each in their turn a labor of love, and they all love and serve well because they love me.† We are all harmony. When things are tough I tell them a story, or propose a tune, and they will sing and work it all through. Abba is very useful; she is our Express from room to room, and old Dr. Ripley, brother of the Concord Patriarch, wrote her an acrostic which has given her great consequence among her fellows. Miss Mary Emerson boards here because she likes the company, but she is [al]most too pungent dose to take every day. She has been made to chew some sour grapes in her past life, and her teeth and temper have her set on edge. At her time of life, 75, *sweetness* is not easily recovered.‡

My house is on the market. We wait for the event. I toil and trust,

---

★Anna Alcott was still teaching in New Hampshire, living with cousins.
†She supervised a staff of women at the spa.
‡Mary Moody Emerson, Ralph Waldo's aunt, resided in Waterford, Maine.

believing more firmly than ever that anxiety fumbleth in the dark, while hope anchors, and looking ever upward waits. I sought for the father but could not find him. I trust and wait and lo! He finds me, finds me. Do I say yes!! He blesses me too, with cheerful heart for each exigency,—*

In June, only a few weeks after arriving at the spa, Abigail decided that its environment was unhealthy for her seven-year-old daughter and sent Abby May home. She kept Eliza Stearns, who was more difficult to manage, and wrote to request "Louisa's company and services at Waterford," as Bronson informed Anna in a letter. "The eager girl will now fly [to Maine] as soon as opportunity and speed shall favor." Before Louisa could set off, however, Abigail became so disillusioned with the spa management that she decided she could no longer remain. She wrote to Louisa bidding her not make the trip, and began arranging to return home herself. She and Eliza left Waterford by stagecoach in early July and arrived in Concord on the 10th or 11th.

To her friend Ann Sargent Gage
of Waterford, Maine

Concord, July 13, 1848

There has been no moment, my dear friend, since my arrival at the threshold of my Home that I could pass with you, even to acknowledge the obligation I am under for your many favours during my sojourn in Waterford—and more especially to return your loan so promptly and kindly extended to me, in money for my passage. I reached home with my helpless charge [Eliza Stearns], and truly glad was I to again find myself in the atmosphere of love and comfort, two essential elements of my being wholly deficient at W[aterford].

I already feel a partial restoration of my wasted energy, and am

---

*The rest of this letter is cut from the bound volume of letters.

more and more convinced that I have infringed too largely on the laws physique of my being, as well as made a greater sacrifice of home and happiness than I can ever be indemnified for, by any association with men and manners such as have presented themselves at W[aterford]. . . . Despair is no paragraph in our chapter for the day. Our lesson is to do, and bear, toil and stress, and though doomed to tread the earth with the earthly, we aspire to carry our heads in the heavens with the heavenly; if we must deal with men, we will take sweet counsel of Angels. What a sweet message in the careless carol of the birds. They take no thought of the morrow. They garner no bread for their journey, yet all are fed. They know that the compassions of the Lord are enduring. And birds would not have them if grains were not scattered by a gracious Providence for their busy bills to gather. I blush to think that it is Man, only man that doubts, and trembles for his substance. Even the Sparrow hath more confiding love in the Creator. If we do not already see our father in the vexations of our life, if we seek him in its distractions but find him not, let us trust and love, and he will find and bless us. Let our feet be found on the mountains to bring glad tidings to the wary, weary and soul-sad; it were well to abide for a time with the Sufferers and labourers if only to feel and rejoice in our Strength and moral might.

I have had a rich experience. . . . But the calm peaceful loveful condition of my home will soon restore the balance of my mind and seared heart.

I hope your daughter from Washington will not fail to give me a call, or inform me of her arrival that I and my daughters may see her.* These dear, these precious jewels in which you and I my dear friend are so regally invested. I always rejoiced over the birth of each girl-child. I never was one as Miss Fuller says "to make the lot of the sex such that mothers must be sad when daughters are born." Oh no! they bring a dower in their love, a purity in their gentle hearts,

---

*Gage's grown daughter was Rowena Coffin Whitman.

which no royal diadem can surpass in nature or brilliancy. They cannot all be Venus's [*sic*] for they are not born of the Graces, but they may all be good for they are loved of God.

Remember me if you please to each and all with fond regard, and believe me yours most gratefully, Abba Alcott

Enclosed within the sum of $5.00—Concord Bank—Abba Alcott

Concord, July 20, 1848

Mrs. Gage, I am somewhat anxious to know if you received a letter from me last week containing $5.00. Please drop me a line by return of Mail.

A lady with her daughter, another with her son both invalids, and two gentlemen are waiting to ascertain if the arrangements at Waterford are competent at all to their comfort and confidence. May I ask the favor of you to ascertain if they have a cook, or a presiding Genius of any sort in the domestic department, to which I can look to secure to them the courtesies and comforts of life. I have hoped that the presence of Dr. Prescott would give dignity and character to the Establishment, the lack of which hitherto has I find been a hindrance to many who wished to enjoy "the Treatment."

My kindest remembrance to your dear circle who are cherished in my remembrance each and all.

Abba Alcott.

Journal entries

September 19, 1848. I have an offer to go as Nurse and companion to a friend of mine to New York for a few weeks. I shall go if she can afford to meet my portions. Anything is better than this. . . .*

---

*She refers to the physical, mental, and financial uncertainty she had experienced in eighteen years of marriage.

Women should strengthen their minds by reflection, 'til their heads become a balance for their hearts. Their actions would be more perpendicular, their whole life more direct and true, not so inclining and vacillating tender and timid. Many of the evils of Woman's life may be traced to the want of education of the *senses*. They do not *see* clearly, hear distinctly, feel

Girls are taught to seem, to appear, not to be and do.

deeply. Thus when they describe anything, they are not quite sure of the distance, or colour; when they tell anything it is quite certain [their] statement is a good deal modified and inaccurate, and their sensations are false or feeble. Girls are taught to *seem,* to appear, not to *be* and *do.* Costume not armour, dress not panoply, is the covering for women. Innocence not virtue, beauty not godliness, should be the foundation of a woman's character.

October 8, 1848. This book given to me on this my 48th birthday I dedicate to the record of my best thoughts during my best hours. Life has many phases to me; only the brightest and best should be stretched on paper. Much of the dark hue takes a tinge from my physical condition, and a morbid sympathy with human suffering. Many of my brighter moments are mere scintillations of hope and joy springing from some unlooked for success or determination to overcome fate by faith. . . .

Louisa wrote the following lines to commemorate my birthday, which she presented me with 2 collars:

Home! Home! hath a blessed sound wherever I may be;
and the sunny hours of a happy youth rise gaily up to me.
Oh, few there are in the great cold world, full as it is of woe,
Who have no place where love can dwell, a home, however low.

To the most forlorn and friendless one will some sweet image come,
Of gentle words and happy hearts, a mother's love and warm home.

There's not a flower in the fields, no green leaves on the tree.
I have nothing but my heart's best love, Mother, to offer thee.

Home again with her family, Abigail still had to solve the problem of how to support them. That fall they moved to a basement apartment in Boston's South End, where they lived among immigrants from Ireland and Germany, free blacks, and fugitive slaves. Abigail, though she was poor herself, had agreed to serve as a "Missionary to the Poor," feeding, clothing, and finding employment for Boston's most needy, paid for by a consortium of wealthy donors.

Journal entry

December 25, Christmas Day. Pass the day, which was wet, dark and dreary, with my family. Hopeful Anna cheering doubting mother. Loving Louisa trying by many quiet acts of comfort to make life more tolerable. Dear Lizzy by her repose and self reliance groping through this mist of things and adverse circumstance. And little Abba a "cricket on the hearth" chirping, free from care or anxiety. Cogswell [her tenant] sends a check for $30 dollars for rent of [Hillside] house at Concord, which we forth-with handed to Mr. Hewes, our landlord [in Boston].

Abigail's new job involved gathering and distributing groceries, clothing, soap, shoes, fuel, and other basic living supplies to the poor of Boston's South End.

Every month or two she wrote a report on her work, which she delivered in person to her sponsors:

Fragments of Abigail's "Reports While Visitor to the Poor of Boston," 1849

Mrs. Alcott's Report, Boston, February 24, 1849. As today completes the first month of my Missionary labors, during which time I have had frequent occasion to call for your alms, as well as counsel, I thought it would not be uninteresting [for you] to hear a brief report of my receipts and expenditures as well as some cases which have come under my care.

In January some of my friends proposed my undertaking this Mission as they thought me well qualified to serve the poor judiciously, and possessing some facilities for communicating their wants to the rich and benevolent. I am secured by their generous contributions in the sum of thirty dollars per month, by which means I am enabled to meet some of the expenses of my family. My heart has always been pledged to the cause of the destitute and oppressed; now my time shall be sacredly devoted to their relief.

Much of the first week was spent in looking up the public records to which I might resort for aid, the overseers of the poor in each ward, the various charitable societies, and benevolent individuals. I also tried to form some plan of operation by which I could serve the poor most effectively and become an intelligent and acceptable medium of communication to the rich, and in every way an agent of relief. How far I have succeeded the Sequel must show. Where I have solicited charity I have (with few exceptions) met with more hospitality than I expected; where I have bestowed charity, I have usually found much greater destitution than I had expected, and the little I had to say, and the very little I could do, was received in the kindest manner and most grateful spirit. To sum up, I have visited 49 paupers, solicited and received

> *To some reading is . . . as important to their moral being as air and light are to their existence.*

aid from 22 persons, called and been refused assistance at 5 places, called and been refused admittance at 9 places. I have solicited money to the amount of $43, have distributed $53. Bed, clothing $14. Rent $9. . . . supplying many articles of clothing, shoes, socks, mittens, hoods, caps, cloaks, frocks, etc. Also distributed 4 bibles and 20 tracts, with as [much] reading as people could appreciate; to some, reading is an element of happiness and as important to their moral being as air and light are to their existence.

Mr. [Theodore] Parker says (most truly) we need the Palliative Charity, and the "Remedial Justice." We do! Most essentially. Do the poor *justice,* and no alms giving would be required. They are treated with too much severity; we induce them to deceive us, for they feel we do not love them. Let us infuse more love into our gift, and it will be doubly blest.

I find most [poor] persons begin by excusing themselves; this should be discouraged by our making a broad excuse for them at once. . . . Believe me, it is more frequent that despair paralyses the heart than that hunger starves the body. We may legislate in wisdom, we may multiply our charity schemes, but never until society looks upon poverty as an incident of man's condition, not as a crime of his nature, shall we see any permanent or beautiful results from our laws or our almsgiving. If we find destitution without sin as its cause or consequence, we should sympathize and relieve it. If we find poverty with sin as its cause, and sorrow its result, we should pity and reform it, in all cases showing a tender but wise mercy.

It requires a probe skillfully guided, to touch our most fatal, but often least apparent disease, not a plaster laid on without a care to heal or a hope to cure. We must lay no soothing unction to this sore spot of our condition. We are becoming centrally diseased. We should study pauperism and crime, as we do any other science so intimately connected with human beings, society, and its laws. . . .

Can we not increase the comfort of the homes of the poor? Can we not spare yet more, and more from our luxuries for their necessities? Oh! Let us listen to the response of our best nature; it surely will be in their behalf.

Mrs. Alcott's report, Boston, spring, 1849 . . . My labours and experience for the past month have been most diversified and interesting. Almsgiving has been less my business than for the few previous months, for one very cogent reason, I have had but few alms to bestow. . . . My labors have been mostly for Americans and Germans, yet no day has passed without my attention and aid having been solicited and given to the Irish (emigrant or sick). I am accosted in the Streets every day by those who having been driven by the fear of famine or oppression have gathered up their last fragment of earthly possession, and find their way here for protection or employment. I cannot pass by; I must whisper a word of encouragement or hope to them, although I feel a sinking sadness tugging at my own anchor. Their life-boat is drifting, a small rope many save it. Throw it in mercy, and all may yet go safely.

I feel quite as much sympathy, perhaps more fear, for that tide of floating humanity who throng our streets on parade every day, whose flag of availability is on her head, whose highest aspiration is a Mantilla, whose last best hope is a *husband*! She dreams that the moment her duties are over in the kitchen, her highest privilege is her Toilette, confident that there she surpasses her Mistress in success, for at her bidding the Graces attend in Legion. . . . Shall we give them more money or fewer temptations? Shall we give her more gold or more education?

. . . This is but an embryo scheme. I hope as it becomes better known and appreciated, I shall have your cooperation and the good will of the Public. In the winter season it can be used as a "relief room" for the Destitute, a council chamber for the Rich, a Bank of Faith for the Doubting, an Anchor of Hope to the Despairing, an Ark of Safety to the friendless, a Bow of promise to the Striving. Let us be steadfast tho' the Ravens fail us, or the heavens fall;

remembering that from small beginnings are often large & lasting results. . . .

To Samuel Joseph

Boston, July 29, [18]49

Dearest brother,

. . . My duties now take me all over the city, as I am duly inaugurated into City mission duty. . . . The office is a laborious one but not new to me in all its departments. I have always felt a care for those more destitute than myself. I am disgusted with the lack of strength and simplicity in our priests and the "ministry at large" is a sinecure. Our charitable societies are too complex, the poor are freezing and starving, while wrapped in our sables and picnicking on tea and toast we discuss resolutions.

. . . I try to get up a more neighborly feeling, and introduce on a small scale the association principle. If one woman has 2 flat irons and one tub [and] her neighbor has 2 tubs and 1 flat iron, I demonstrate to them the economy and gain by interchanging their tools. . . . And now the flats and tubs circulate hot and thick all up and down. . . . Love is economical as well as beautiful. . . .

Dear Sam, from all I hear you are far from comfortable. Don't attempt to do so much for others. It is better that each should carry his own load than that you should bear a part of all. . . .

Anna is passing the winter [in Boston] with Louisa Bond and keeping school for hers and the neighbor's children. Louisa is keeping house for me. Elizabeth and Abba go to [the school of] Miss Peabody and so we are disposed of by Providence and by destiny, but anything is better than stagnation or discontent.

Yrs, dear Sam, as ever, Abba

Fragments of "Reports While Visitor to the Poor," 1849–1850

Mrs. Alcott's Report, Relief Room at 698 Washington St., Boston, October 18, 1849. Ladies . . . I am desirous of suggesting also a sewing class to meet Wednesday afternoons. Our public schools overlook this part of female education or they leave it wholly unprovided for. Many a girl can wield a pen or calculate a sum, who can do nothing with a needle, that little instrument, so important to a woman through life, indeed almost the only tool vouchsafed to her, but which she can obtain a subsistence. The free and skillful use of that leads to habits of patient industry, to order and neatness. They might be taught to mend the garments and sew for the charity basket. Teach them to hem-gauge, hem, make buttonholes, and darn stockings.

Reading and writing are important to every human being but sewing is an indispensible *art*. A woman can take no very respectable situation in society as an operative who cannot mend or make clothing. Skillful in that, she need not want for occupation the most agreeable and with some exceptions the most profitable. I often observe where there is no needle work there is the most shiftlessness and ennui. Among the poor you will generally find most contentment and least vice where the mother . . . is a needle-woman.

I hope a sewing-machine will never be invented; it is the perfect machine of the old countries that has reduced its millions to destitution and despair. A more equal division of labour, the domestic arts and moral sciences, would

My mind and heart have always toiled for the oppressed.

have produced very different results. Governments, politics, morals and religion are essentially modified by the culmination of the domestic arts. . . .

And if agreeable and unanimous is your choice to continue me as your agent, . . . I shall be happy to do so for the ensuing 6 months. I shirk at no physical exertion. My mind and heart have always toiled for the oppressed. I have volunteered the work of missionary for many years, and the only sad feature about my present position is the necessity I am under of accepting compensation. But years have multiplied upon me, my family tho' not numerous is somewhat dependant. I am a wife, mother, and native citizen of Boston. My services shall be conscientiously performed. Your wages shall be fully earned. Ladies, I await any instructions you may have to give, either collectively or individually—*

Mrs. Alcott's Report, January 3, 1850. Ladies! Permit me to offer you the congratulations of the season, a carol for Merry Christmas, a hearty good wish for health and happiness in the new year. Amidst its courtesies and festivities, I know you have not forgotten the cause to which we are pledged, and I trust we are ready to renew our obligations to the Poor and each other. Let us for a few moments review the past, and suggest for the future; see where we can exalt a motive or apply a principle.

Your Basket, the Poor's Purse, my own solicitations for charity, have enabled us to give much relief, but the demands are so numerous, our charity so popular, our ability so much exaggerated that whenever I have set aside a case as not within my power to aid, it has caused great dissatisfaction to those who have applied for relief. I am too often compelled to say no, . . . and am sure I leave a hard thought on the mind as well as bitter word on the lips. And in most cases, explanation or reasoning has been of no avail; I have had an abundance of censure from the rich, misrepresentation by the poor. Mine is no enviable position.

. . . I go with my daughter 3 evenings in the week to teach a class of colored adults. This much neglected class of native Americans

---

*Note ends abruptly because document is cut.

should not be so forgotten by our philanthropists. . . . Our colored people, their very skin a cross, bear quietly the apprehension which prejudice heaps upon them. Occasionally you hear of them, through the notoriety of a Quincy or a Sumner who dares to plead their rights in a court of justice. Yes, law must decide if they sit on a bench under the same roof with our children to learn their primer or their Bible. Our religion has turned them from our altars, but we dare not defy the Laws of Man tho' we disobey every command of God. . . .

Mrs. Alcott's Report, February 7, 1850. Ladies, I will interrupt your social enjoyment this evening as little as possible although I have allowed myself to feel a sort of right to your attention on these occasions, as none other has been offered me, to communicate. . . .

Our charities are ample, but our arrangements are inadequate. The 40 organized benevolent societies or associations for relief . . . cross each other's purposes, sadly enough making the unfortunate, helpless, and the cunning still more treacherous. . . .

Our Sisters of Charity get dog-weary with this nonsense; if they are not always as amiable as angels, it is because angels have wings and are not subject to old legs and new shoes. It is this shiftlessness, this non-get-at-ableness, that throws me into splenetic humor, with our institutions, charities, and philanthropies. . . .

Our relief Room . . . was [created] in the hope that on a humble scale, with wise coadjutors, intelligent counselors, and loving friends, at my room (*the* room rather, for I hoped it would be more yours than mine); it was in view of all these advantages . . . that I proposed working for Ward No. 11, to have a place where poor and rich could be put in communication without much loss of time, mind, or money; a kind of neutral ground, a receptacle for your surplus substance, and a source from which your organized charities might flow. Various causes however seemed to disappoint me, and my aspirations after a model-room, is likely I think

to prove a "loophole of retreat" for the indolent, a room of con-
tention to the applicants, as well as a hindrance and Mar-Plot to
your Agent.

. . . The order of 30 dollars, which Mr. Mayo so generously gave
me, I could not conscientiously occupy, as it is one way I enter my
protest against the use of spirituous liquors, not to patronize the
seller.* The traffic in liquor is degrading to the vender and destructive to the buyer. Witnessing as I do the poverty, crime, and despair
resulting in the too free use of intoxicating liquors, I will never
knowingly send a person where it can be had on any pretext.

Cold-water is always better than rum on a sore leg. Cold-water is
always better on an aching head than cologne-water (which means
scented alcohol). So entirely do I believe in its salutary power over
all disease, that if agreeable arrangements can be made for my family, I hope to be elected the Prima-Donna of a Water Cure, to
which, Ladies, in your summer rustication, I invite you most cor-
dially to call. You shall each and all be welcome to a plunge, spray,
or shower-bath and a brisk rub with a crash-mitten—the best of all
remedies for warm talks and cool friendships.

Respectfully submitted, Abba Alcott

March 1850. Ladies, the winter is over but not gone. The spring
has come, but is not here. The singing of birds, blooming flowers, and playing of fountains will soon greet us as harbingers of all-
delicious summer.

But cheering and charming as all this is, my friends, perhaps
there is no one cause of pleasure and gratitude more real and enduring than that of having diffused comfort, relieved want, imparted
sympathy to the sorrowing. These outward and natural pleasures
we ought to enjoy and be grateful for, but the remembrance of

---

*Her daughter Anna added later, "The order was for groceries at a shop where
liquor was sold; Mother wouldn't accept it."

well-done duties brings with it a satisfaction to the heart, a contentment and repose to the soul, which throws about our daily life a
peace and joy magical as birds, odorous as flowers, brilliant as June,
and refreshing as fountains. . . .

You have come together this evening, my friends, to sew for the
poor, like good Dorcas's [*sic*] to make garments for the naked. This
is praise-worthy, but it is not incompatible with the swiftest stitch-
ing, to deliberate well the principle which moves you to this labor,
or the object you would promote—the "cause of Pauperism" and
the best means for its prevention. For while we are doing the one,
the other need not necessarily be left undone. And while you seek
light to thread your needles, and patterns to shape your garments,
let me help to open the shutters and spread the fabric of our social
arrangements. We are all part and parcel of this condition of things,
and *I* for one am a restless fragment and can't find my niche. I know
I belong somewhere, and in trying to find my place I am constantly
jostling those who are on the same search. . . .

We do a good work when we clothe the Poor. We do a better
one when we make the way easy for them to clothe themselves. We
shall do the best thing when we so arrange society as to *have no Poor.*

Mrs. Alcott's report, Boston, April 1850. Ladies! The term of six
months for which I was engaged as your agent and almoner having expired with the month of March, I thought it might be most
satisfactory to you to have an elaborate detail of my labors; what I
have received, what and how expended, whom I have relieved. . . .
A large amount of my work has been almsgiving. It is true I have
been compelled to do more of this than I desired, for in my opinion
it is the least expedient way of relieving wants, and the most certain
method of superinducing pauperism. . . .

I certainly would not increase your fears of imposition or discourage your sharing lovingly the good things of life, with the needy
and wretched. But simple almsgiving pledges a man to the abuses

of society. A gift bestowed by request should always be accompanied with a regret from the giver that it is *not more,* never with a
reproof that it is not deserved. Forbear giving, but never reproach
the receiver. Give of your substance cheerfully but with discrimination, and feel not quite content until the necessity for asking has in
some measure been removed. . . .

I have spoken of employment as the only efficient remedy for
destitution. Employ, but pay well. Give of your substance cheerfully, but with discrimination, and feel not quite content till the
necessity for asking has in some measure been obviated.

That is the only efficient charity which helps to remove the
causes of poverty, not that temporary relief of the symptoms of
want. . . . Every day of my life and every experience of my life (&
it is one full of event), convinces me that our social arrangements,
that is, our selfish and isolated households, which by a strange mis-
nomer are called social arrangements, are at the foundation of all
our great social evils. Did the law of love prevail, and that is the
law of universal providence, then we should all be provided for
without anxiety, without loss of time or spirit. Now because some
want so much, many cannot have any. A few want all, some get
nothing.* Some produce, others consume. Some get, others spend.
Many suffer. . . .

Employment is needed, but just compensation is more needed.
Is it not inhuman to task a man's strength to his uttermost by all
sorts of competition. . . . Alas for the laborer. . . . He may receive
good wages in money, but he soon finds himself bankrupt in health
and energy. And woman too. How often I am told as an apology for
exquisite and extra stitches that it "furnishes employment for the
poor." This hackneyed, this selfish apology . . . can no longer shield

---

*Abigail wrote, "Most get nothing," then crossed out "most" and replaced it
with "some."

the miserable vanity that can only find gratification in the servitude of numerous fellow beings.

Advertisement by Abigail, 1850

The Relief Room, 12 Groton Street. The Subscriber earnestly solicits your aid to her Mission, by sending to this Room contributions, however small, of clothing, shoes, socks, bonnets, hoods, hats, old flannels and Linens also, patches of any material, and linings; orders for groceries, small parcels of soap, and other family necessaries. . . . Best German, American, and . . . Irish help procured at the shortest notice.

Abba Alcott, Missionary

Like their mother, the teenagers Louisa and Anna did all they could to fill the family coffers, teaching, sewing, washing and cleaning, and (in Louisa's case) writing. One of the many domestic jobs Louisa took was as a house servant to a lawyer and his invalid sister. Not only did Mr. Richardson, the lawyer, not produce the promised salary, but also he attempted to seduce seventeen-year-old Louisa. Disgusted, she returned home after seven weeks.

Journal entry

January 11, 1850. Louisa returns from her term [with the Richardsons] after an absence of seven weeks. . . . She is *not* to recognize service, and I am glad the connexion was so loosely sustained, so soon dissolved.

I believe there are some natures too noble to curb, too lofty to bend. Of such is my Lu.

To Samuel Joseph

Boston, February 28th, 1851

My dear S[am],

. . . My business is full of responsibilities, and petty perplexities, hardly giving me 5 c[en]ts a day. Anna is with the Minors. Louisa has gone to do the housework for a small family at Dedham, but every instinct of her being revolts at it, and I am not sure how long she will remain. Elizabeth is doing my housework with the help of Grandma [Alcott,] who is teaching her to cook. And Abba goes to school and is a very fine girl. She has just had mumps and measles but with abundance of water got through very comfortably. Mr. Alcott has been solicited to continue by "readings and conversations on the ancient poets and philosophers" which he will do. . . .

Our papers keep you informed of the stormy times here. Never was a darker day in our country's history.* I have sent 20 colored women to service in the country, where for the present they will be safe; [but] may yet have to meet the penalties of the law. I am ready and willing. There are higher laws the infringement of which I fear more.

There is a great inconsistency in the manners and methods of the abolitionist. They want a larger infusion of love, and a softer clearer light. If Edmund Quincy "pshaws" in a lady's face he must expect that his glasses will be smeared with unsaleable eggs; we always get as good as we send. There is no courtesy among them, and some of their meetings are a practical lie. And George Thompson will never be listened to until he wipes his nose clear of snuff and his mouth clear of froth.†

----

*In 1850 Congress had severely strengthened the Fugitive Slave Act, requiring all American citizens, including those in free states, to capture runaway slaves and return them to their owners.

†Thompson was a famous English abolitionist. Edmund Quincy was one of Abigail's abolitionist cousins.

Boston, April 28, 1851

My dear Brother, I often feel a yearning desire to write you, during these intensely interesting times, but my business is so absorbing both of time and mind. . . . My life is one of daily protest against the oppression and abuses of society. I find selfishness, meanness, . . . contemptible action among people

My life is one of daily protest against the oppression and abuses of society.

who fill high places in church and state; the whole system of servitude in New England is almost as false as slavery in the South. It certainly is as fatal to the moral and religious perceptions . . . Charles Sumner's election is certainly encouraging. . . .

The descendants of devout Puritans, Abigail's relatives and friends reserved the Sabbath for prayer, religious devotions, and rest. She and her daughters, however, were more relaxed about this custom, as she explained in a letter to her brother Samuel Joseph amid the conflict over the Fugitive Slave Law.

Boston, November 10, 1851

. . . There is a terrible strife here, and much oppression in various ways enacted on those who talk of higher laws than human policy. But I shall have my confidence shaken in the supervision of a just God if Daniel Webster and his machinery are to much longer work the destinies of this nation. . . . We may not live to see slavery done away with at the South, but we shall see very soon that Fugitive Slave Law repealed. Let us then pray for repeal, work for repeal. . . .

Thank dear Charlotte for her letter. Louisa will muster courage to tell her own story soon. I have had some regret at allowing Charlotte to sew on Sunday, as she never had done it before. Not that I feel any doubt about the righteousness of it for myself, if I did I should cease. And never should have permitted my girls to do it. I am often obliged to wash for a few hours on Sunday morning that I may get through on Monday. . . . There is often a beautiful worship in labor on the Sabbath. I would not do away the institution but I cannot always comply with the requirements of society in regard to the manner of using it. I feel most near the divine when in the fullest accomplishment of my human relations. I must work or my family suffer, and my present occupation gives me such fragments of days that I am compelled to labor while others rest. My days for service are numbered, and when summoned I shall at least not be found rusty for lack of use. There will be great comfort in that summing up the Life Record.

Boston, February 13, 1852

My dear brother, I have just received your draft for twenty-five dollars which I suppose you intended for I need not reiterate. Dear S, I have often said before to you that it is most painful to be under these obligations, but what can I do? It is something that my courage is not all paralyzed, for fate now in its discipline has not wholly cramped my resolution. I am not bought [or] sold (thank God) [nor] am I driven from the consolations of a benign husband and affectionate daughters, but society is antagonism, with all my ideas of justice and righteousness, and will freeze, starve, and coerce us for our rectitude. Where is the sympathy? Where the abolitionism to emancipate patient trusting souls from this state of bondage?

Boston, October 3, 1852

. . . I am suffering from an exceptional accumulation of fat. I am very corpulent, and lethargic. I have very little opportunity for exercise. I have only left the city for a few hours this summer. That was on the occasion of the funeral of Louisa Bond's dear little boy. . . .

Thank Lotty* for her music book and also for her suggestions for

---

*A nickname for her niece Charlotte May.

Louisa. I am sure if "Fanny Fern" is popular Louisa would receive premiums as thick as blackberries.* However L[ouisa]'s genius works best when least invoked. I have been trying to persuade her and Anna to add a few lines to Lotty; this they decidedly refuse to do. They are both out of employment and I am anxious about their arrangements for winter. Anna is not in firm health. Lizzy and Abba are going to school. I am continuing in my office. My business increases rapidly, but I am not content at my receipts or position. But *doomed* souls should resist as little as possible. The less they aspire, or resist, the less painful is their fate. . . . Life is full of strangeness. To some the full stream of plenty may only touch parched lips.†

In late October 1852, with the money Abigail received from Nathaniel Hawthorne for Hillside House, the Alcotts removed to a rented townhouse on Boston's Beacon Hill, where they would remain for more than two years.

To Samuel Joseph

Pinckney Street, December 14, 1852

My dear S[am], I was glad to get your letter, and truly rejoiced to find you so encouraged about Lucretia.‡ Change of air, diet, external influence will do much to restore her tone of stomach and nervous energy. . . .

I hope Joseph will make free with our house.§ He must feel that

---

*"Fanny Fern" was the pen name of an extremely popular writer for women and children.

†The remainder of this letter was excised.

‡Lucretia May was suffering from dyspepsia.

§Samuel Joseph's son Joseph was now a student at Harvard College, and he often stayed with the Alcotts at 20 Pinckney Street.

tho' humble we have a world of comfort, and that I can sew for him or care for him while at Cambridge, and in doing all I can it will be but a small return for all his father and mother have done for me and mine. *Impress this upon him.* The girls have been terribly destitute of clothing and Mr. A[lcott] is too shabby for decency. . . . Louisa has 6 scholars and Anna is going to assist Elizabeth Sullivan at her school under Park Street; she will give her 4 or 5 doll[ar]s a week. . . . [Elizabeth Sullivan] will be of great use to Anna who can be studying under her direction and perhaps ultimately assume the whole school. My Lizzy is going the 1st of Jan[uar]y to the City Normal School and Abby to the Model School. . . . The housework, cooking, washing, and ironing I shall do myself. . . . I feel better for working about, and it is more respectable to be *in* my family than a servant of the public in any capacity. Society is a humbug, and to be *used by* it, in any way, is *ignoble.* I hate to be even remotely accepting of the false relations of Mistress and Maid. . . .

My dear S, I seem to be wandering off, but I am in the traces, and in seeking about for what is to be done I am horror stricken at the multiplied obstacles to an honest livelihood. Time may modify and simplify this for us, but the present aspect is most discouraging.

I think Mr. Hawthorne will not refuse to pay for the land.* It is announced that Gen. Pierce will give him a fat office in return for his Biographical Sketch.† G. Curtis has got out a Book [on] "Houses of American Authors." Mr. Hawthorne's 2 Concord residences are given, Mr. Emerson's, and all the summer houses of Mr. A[lcott]'s building, whom he honors with the title of Plato. . . . There are good

---

*Hawthorne was negotiating with Abigail to buy land surrounding Hillside House.

†Hawthorne was writing a sketch of his close friend General Franklin Pierce, who in 1853 would become president.

bits of Transcendental aspiration, but a great lack of reverence of goodness and wisdom. But this is not a reverential age!!

January 2, 1853

. . . I am just getting over an attack of mumps, not severe. The girls enjoy it much when Mother has to keep still. It's beautiful to have the fat old Lady keep quiet.

Abby begins tomorrow at the Bowdoin School, Myrtle St. I mean to have her fairly harnessed into a common school drill.

I am beginning the new year nearly out of debt, of course out of danger, and am in hope that fortune will favor us with her smiles, if nothing more to keep us in heart a few years longer.

Boston [Pinckney Street] March 19, 1853

[Our life in Boston] is not as productive as I would wish. Still, it is an advance on the past struggling, scratching for a subsistence. It is all on a higher plane of action, and it is everything to keep these girls *up,* up. Too many are down because they

I say to all the dear girls, keep up, *be something in* yourself.

lose sight of their *rights,* and ask . . . as a favour for that which should be given *gratuitously.* Too few think deep[ly] enough. Out of all this shallowness and frivolity, how can substance come? . . .

Women have protested well against their wrongs, but do they *know* their *best* rights, the right to *think, feel,* and *live* individually in an exalted state? I say to all the dear girls, keep *up,* be something in *yourself.* Let the world feel at some stage of its diurnal revolution that you are on its surface, *alive,* not in its bowels a dead decaying *thing.* . . .

Yrs. Abba A.

In the early 1850s, women began petitioning state legislatures for the right to vote. Abigail authored a petition in her rented townhouse.

Petition to the Massachusetts Legislature
for Female Suffrage, 1853

We . . . women of Massachusetts as aforesaid, do respectfully request the Constitutional Convention now in session to ordain that, when the said amendments and alterations are submitted to the People for their ratification and adoption, all women, residents of the Commonwealth, who have attained the full age of twenty-one years, shall be entitled to vote on the same, and that their votes shall be counted as of equal value and potency with those of men. And we submit this request, in order that in case our power to govern ourselves shall be deemed to be transferred out of our own hands, where it naturally belongs, it may be so transferred by our consent and in order also that the government of the Commonwealth may really be constituted by the consent of the governed.

The Legislature rejected the petition.

To Louisa May Alcott, age eighteen

Boston, July 4, 1853

I am pleased to hear you say that your mind is quite as ease, and [that] you get happiness out of writing and reading letters. Your summer will, I am sure, have been well and profitably spent, and you will feel a joy at the strength of purpose which bid you the effort; your friends all respect you for the [illegible] and honorable exertions which you are both making to assist the family.

Keep up dearest! Get all the enjoyment you can from intercourse with others, but your best and most enduring, will be that of your own character, motives, &c.

Elizabeth says you send all the beams★ to Anna. I am willing if you will send such nice notes to us. You write remarkably well, and the hand part of it, we can forgive because the head part is so good.

In 1853 Abigail learned that her much older brother Charles was having marital troubles.

To Samuel Joseph

September 4, 1853

My dear brother . . . The fact is, Charles has never given up drinking occasionally, and after 6 weeks of sleepless night[s], anxious wretched day[s], what more could be expected of a man whose animal nature has always preponderated. I pity the man from my soul. His task with his wife has been fraught with trial, [she is] a very diseased person, highly irritable, at times petulant and exacting. Charles has suffered in many ways, but he is a facile person with an easy conscience, who can never forgive the past, is discontented with the present, and defies the future. The times are against him. He has too much sentiment and too little enterprise for this age, the silver and gold age, the age of revenue and political economy. Such men as Mr. Alcott with his idealism and philosophy and Charles with his sophistry and sentiment perish in such latitudes of the world. But they have their virtues and must not be left to perish. I believe the former is imperishable and will survive in a posthumous reputation that is known to few in this period of the world.

Let me advise that you leave Charles to his wife. . . . She will not let him suffer. . . . Write Charles an encouraging kind letter,

---

★"Gossip," according to a note penciled in later by Louisa.

but don't hint at the separation; let that come from his wife. If she chooses to take her child to Lynn [Massachusetts] to pass the winter with her parents, they will promote it. They [Charles and his wife] can let their place very well and Charles can find some employment in Lynn perhaps. Nobody here knows anything about what has occurred, and the less said the better. . . .

Our girls are pledged to community life somewhere; the world or society as it is now constituted has no attractions for them, and yet they are very social. Anna is the gentlest most lovable being, but quite unobtrusive. She has had a sweet time at Walpole and is much happier . . . and home has fewer attractions than ever as labour with many privations and some hardships is the only promise winter makes us in prospect. Lizzy and Louisa are rather higher metal and their mother is true steel on the labour movement, and their Father's divine element comes in too to dignify and adorn the rough condition of our present life, but Anna suffers where there is not order, gentles and genteel surroundings. . . .

Yrs ever, Abby

Journal entries

December 25, 1853. I am inclined to think the approaching crisis in women's destiny will find a place of no mean magnitude for [Louisa].

January 1, 1854. I have missed the pleasure [of journal writing] at times exceedingly, but my occupations were so constant, often oppressive, that I thought it best to discontinue that which I could not do well. But I resume it from a conviction that it is important to . . . note down not perhaps so

I wish women displayed more brains and less jewelry.

much what happens to us, as what good I may be realizing from my readings or doings. . . .

January 3 . . . Love is the powerful agent to discipline children with.

Boston, 1854. I wish women displayed more brains and less jewelry.

Late Middle Age

*B*y the mid-1850s, after six years in Boston, Abigail could no longer afford to live in the city. Her two older daughters were in their early twenties, Elizabeth nearly twenty, and Abby a young teenager. Anna and Louisa had started a school at home and enjoyed some success as teachers. Louisa also continued to write stories and was working on a book. Despite what they earned and "a handsome bequest of $500 doll[ar]s from my Aunt Davenport's will" in 1854, Abigail could not keep up with her rent on Pinckney Street. Once again she needed a cheaper place to live. Her brother-in-law Benjamin Willis, the wealthy widower of her sister Eliza, offered Abigail a house and garden in Walpole, New Hampshire, rent-free. The Alcotts moved there in May 1855. Her two younger daughters soon contracted scarlet fever.

To Samuel Joseph

February 3, 1855

My dear brother, . . . [I seek a place where] Abby can be educated . . . Louisa can labor and write, Anna labor and teach, Lizzy labor and sew, and I can labor some and take . . . the detail of care which are more annoying to young people.

Mr. Alcott thinks of passing the summer at Plymouth to build a garden house for Mr. Watson, or he will go to England in May. He doesn't wish the latter to be spoken of, but I act on the present with no reference to him. . . .

I suppose father's legacy is nearly gone. I wish you would ascertain for me of S.E. Sewall what the balance is in his hand. It would be a great relief to know. . . . I have drawn largely on it, determined to see this experiment of the school through for 3 winters.* They have 9 scholars but they all go into the country in May, that leaves no more income from the school till next January.

Walpole, [New Hampshire,] May 4, 1855

[I will work] a few more years for the sake of these dear girls, and then my work is done. I know I can be spared. My life has been one of great vicissitude. Its changes and chances are full of discipline and soul conquest. The surrender is nearly accomplished and then I suppose the victory is won. The great questions of right and wrong, of expedient right and necessary wrong, have always puzzled me. The world is full of inconsistency. Men have multiplied laws of action till they have practically proved themselves either knaves or fools, good politicians but bad Christians. This world and its things, are the present basis of all good. . . . We shall see who is right one of these days.[†]

July 29, 1855

My dear brother . . . You may have heard how very sick my Lizzy has been. Scarlet fever took us all down in its various stages of virulence, but it fixed on Lizzy most tenaciously and her father and I watch her night and day with an anxiety most painful and intense, but she is [gaining] strength. . . . If Louisa can be better paid for her labours and Mr A[lcott] can secure one or two hundred each winter, we can get along very well. . . .

Abigail's next trial was to care for her daughter Lizzy, who failed to recover from the scarlet fever she contracted that summer.

---

*Anna and Louisa's school.
[†]She added later, "Questions in Ethics on which wiser heads have been puzzled."

October 9, 1855

Dear S[am],

. . . Oh the past, how full of bitterness, the present how bound by circumstance, the future how impenetrably gloomy and cold. I must leave in sadness but will soon feel better, Abby

To her niece Louisa Willis Wells
on turning ten

Walpole, New Hampshire, [January] 1856

Dear Louisa,

Accept this jewel, a mother's brightest gem, which she first wears on her heart; then in her bosom; then in her crown, From Aunty

> *A happy "New Year"*
> *To my Lu Lu dear;*
> *May joy abound*
> *And love profound*
> *Crown all the days*
> *Of '56*
>
> *May the love of duty,*
> *That charm of beauty;*
> *That light of life,*
> *All peace, no strife,*
> *Guide all your ways*
> *Through '56*
>
> *Pay no regard,*
> *To studies hard;*
> *But work away,*
> *For Time don't stay*

> *To help us through*
> *1856.*
>
> *Love to Father, Mother*
> *Uncle, Sister, Brother,*
> *Grandpa! And Ann too*
> *So kind, So true*
> *And may heavenly dew*
> *Nourish my little "Lu"*
> *Through 56.* ★

Nursing her daughter Elizabeth became the focus of Abigail's life. She con-
sulted with many doctors, but Lizzy still weakened. In the fall of 1857, at
Bronson's urging, Abigail moved back to Concord. Not long afterward, doc-
tors told her Lizzy's case was hopeless. Abigail summoned Bronson home
from his annual western tour in January 1858 and spent the following six
weeks at her twenty-two-year-old daughter's bedside.

To Samuel Joseph

Concord, January 21, 1858

My dear brother, I can lay no purer offering on the Altar of the
Lord than this gentle Spirit. I have struggled to save her for the past
year; but sometimes before our greatest peace comes our hardest
strife, and I now feel that my darling will be in safer hands than her
Mother's. She wrote in my Journal that beautiful Hymn of aspiration by Miss Flower, "Nearer my God to thee." . . .

★Louisa Wells later wrote, "Ann was our good Scotch maid. This letter was sent
me on my 10th Birthday with a daguerreotype of Cousin Louisa [May] Alcott."

Elizabeth Sewall Alcott, twenty-two, died in her mother's arms on March 14, 1858. Samuel Joseph, traveling in Rome, could not preside at her funeral.

To Samuel Joseph

Concord, March 19, 1858

In the anguish of a bereaved heart we are apt to cry out for help. The body sickens and the soul saddens. We seek sympathy and received demonstrations that our friends are with us in our trouble. . . . I dare not dwell on the fever which I conveyed to my home which devoured the freshness of her life, and left her wrecked humanity on the shore of Time for a brief space.* I dare not dwell on the helplessness of science which in the person of four "skillful Drs" I summoned to her aid. The fact is before me, she has faded like a shadow through the valley of death into life and light. She took her form, but has left her influence so powerfully, it is almost a substance. . . .

On Friday evening she reached her arms out of bed to her Father and said take me father into your lap. He did so, bracing himself in the large chair. I took her feet in my lap. The girls, seeing something unusually serene about us, closed in the group. She smiled, looked at each one, "All of us here." She put a stray bleached lock of her father's hair behind his ear. "How beautiful . . . Air, Air." The window was opened. "Heavenly air. I go! I go! Lay me down gently." We did. She slept four hours quietly. To my apprehension it was then she resigned her spirit. After that came physical distress, and all of Saturday ether and wine soothed occasional paroxysms of distress. At 1 Sunday morning I called Anna from the couch, at 2 sent

---

*Abigail and her family suspected they had contracted scarlet fever from a poor family she had fed on her front lawn in Walpole, New Hampshire.

up for Louisa and Abby. We watched the slow receding of all the mortal that was visible till dawn. Louisa and I then laid her dressed on the couch, a form chiseled in Bone, held by a mere integument of skin, no flesh perceptible. Her father came [and said,] "My child, how beautiful." The girls went to bed, and Mr. A[lcott] and myself sat down to try to bring home the lesson.

The winter has been a book of revelations to us. Each day Lizzy has turned a new leaf for our book. May we learn it, and render in our future life the fact that we are wiser for her life, holier for her death.

Journal entries

[1858.] [It has been] an eventful year to us all, but not without its lessons or tests of our faith. When with my sick dying daughter I turned my back forever on [New Hampshire and] its beautiful hills, I felt that although the pastures were green and the hills were covered with the flocks and herds of rich men, I had no bread or honey. For my daughters, I was left to dig or die. . . . I took faithful care of my darling Lizzie till she [was] released from her sufferings by the great Physician of all our woes. . . . She lingered until 1858 March 14th and quietly passed away. This has been to me the inexplicable trial of my life. . . .

1859. For 40 years my father was closely associated with Dr. Freeman as Warden of Stone Chapel.* Our family were baptized, married and buried from that Altar. I have many tender sweet memories with this Church and its functionaries. . . .

January 17, 1860. Louisa and Abby [May] go to Boston for a few

---

*Beside this entry she pasted a newspaper clipping about a celebration of the hundredth anniversary of the birth of the Rev. James Freeman, former minister at King's Chapel, Boston, and a close friend of her father.

weeks. Louisa hears pleasant news. Her story of "Love and Self-love" is accepted by the "Atlantic Monthly." She has reason to be encouraged for the censorship of the "Atlantic" is of no mean order. Her success with her newspaper stories has been quite good; and I am not sure, but this exercise has matured her powers for this last best effort. Her creative as well as descriptive faculties are quite remarkable. She gives you the natural common traits and incidents without any of the vulgar shades which it is so difficult to avoid in picturing rural life or every day scene. Perhaps her shades are a little too dark, tragic; her light a beam too rosy.★

To Samuel Joseph

March 1860, n.d.

[Louisa and May] both seem to have risen a peg or two since one can write for the "Atlantic" and the other dipped so decidedly into the depths of the fine arts. . . .

To Wendell Phillips†

Concord, March 15, [18]60

Wendell Phillips Esq,
Essex St. Boston, Mass

D[ea]r Sir,
My daughter [Louisa] having written a story suggested by your remanding of your own at the late anti-slavery Convention offered

---

★Abigail added later, "Good criticism, Haha!"
†Phillips was a prominent lawyer and abolitionist.

it to a popular magazine for inspection. It was repulsed as being prejudicial to its "interests" although this journal has withunto been quite fragrant of anti-slavery odour. May I ask the favor if with your conscience to forward it to the anti-slavery standard and hoping they may find it worthy [of] printing and praying for, believing that a clip from freedoms three can be floated into safe waters by so imperial a pilot.

Most respectfully, Abby Alcott

On May 23, 1860, at the Alcotts' new home, which Bronson called Orchard House, Anna Alcott was married to John Pratt, of Concord. The couple moved to Chelsea, just north of Boston, and in the coming years had two sons, Freddy and Johnny.

May 23, 1860. May she [Anna] find herself fully possessed of the strength, endurance, all abiding love, to meet the exigencies and aspirations of wedded life.

May 24. AntiSlavery society met here, 42 present. My brother held a discussion on non-resistance [with] Mr. Emerson, Sanborn, Miss Peabody, and Mr. Alcott.★ The widows of John and Watson Brown were here. . . .†

May 29 . . . I prepare for Boston to make my first visit to dear Anna's home, Chelsea.

May 31 . . . Louisa pays our grocer Hastings $50, Also a ton of coal $7.50 . . .

★Franklin Sanborn was a Concord schoolteacher and abolitionist.

†John Brown, a radical abolitionist, had in 1859 led a bloody raid on the U.S. armory in Harpers Ferry, Virginia. He had been captured, been found guilty of treason, rebellion, and first-degree murder, and been hanged. He was now seen as a martyr for the antislavery cause.

To Samuel Joseph

September 8, 1860

. . . I stand as much out of the way [of my daughters] and try to keep myself from being a hindrance to these girls, who are full of life, aspiration, tact and talent. I will never impose my experience upon them as the better guide or wisest way, tho' 30–40 years of a most varied life gives me an accumulated knowledge of the world and its requirements. Bonnie★ will find his way into the substantial good if you only beckon up higher! My boy, up higher! The human soul naturally takes wings if we only don't *clog, curb,* restrain it out of its upward tendencies. Encouragement and the example of our own best life is our greatest responsibility. Influence is better than precept, and when we insinuate by the sweetness of our own life, that goodness into our children which we most desire them to profess, we have done more than schools, and all that Heaven can require of us as parents. . . .

Journal entries

January or February 1861 . . . Anna seems quite happy . . . Abby [May] writes in fine spirit, takes air, exercise every day; seems pleased with her employment as teacher at the Idiot Asylum [at] Syracuse.† Sees something of general society and her Uncle's family. . . . Louisa finds some time for writing, but my frequent sick-turns interrupt her too much. It is with real sorrow I find her

---

★Samuel Joseph's son George.

†Anna Alcott had taught for several years in the 1850s at an asylum run by a friend of her uncle Samuel Joseph in Syracuse, where May now taught art. Both Alcotts boarded with their uncle and aunt.

compelled by circumstances to leave her desk for the kitchen, but life is full of sacrifice for women.

We need more money; how and where it is to be obtained seems quite uncertain. My health is not firm, and my heart less valiant.

March 3, 1861, Sunday. Many interruptions through the day prevented my writing [in my journal]. I love to record something at least once a week. A life seems but half lived if no record of thought or motive be made visible; it helps memory. Even the best of us are forgotten soon enough; let us perpetuate in the remembrances of our children at least, what of love and good-will we have lived for them, what at such a period of our life we were reading, thinking or proposing to do—what we were hoping, desiring, believing. As I sometimes take up an old Diary of mine, I am encouraged to believe these records are not without their value. At times I have written but little, and I miss the data very much.

Monday, March 18, 1861. I daily pray for health and courage to sustain them [Louisa and Bronson] in their efforts, if I am past making any myself to redeem the apparent inertness and helplessness of the family. A little more money, fewer wants, or better economy would free us from dependance or obligation.

When the Civil War began, in April 1861, two of John Brown's daughters were staying with Abigail and her family in Concord.

To Samuel Joseph

April 14, 1861

Are we not beginning to reap in the storm what was there sown in the whirlwind? I dread a war, but is not a peace based on such false compromises and compacts much more disastrous to the real prospects of the country generally, and Freedom in particular? I think so. If the Border States secede, they may ship us at the North

but I think we can call in aid from foreign powers, and may yet sub-
jugate the whole brood South and Border.★

Journal entry

October 8, 1861.† [I] Received . . . from Louisa a nice hair brush . . .
my day was past [*sic*] tranquilly almost sadly. I thought much of how
little I had been to this family, and really how little I was in myself.
Then I soothed this state of discontent by reassuring myself how hard
I had tried to bear up against the adverse of life and make the most
of all that was agreeable, or successful, and closed the day in devout
thankfulness that courage alone defeats the onsets of misfortune, and
often by bearing cheerfully we overcome the evil we dread.

Abigail pasted in her journal this birthday letter from Louisa.

Dearest Marmee,
   It has troubled me for a long while to see such an old brush on
the toilette table of the lady who possessed the handsomest head of
hair in the house, so here is a new one with loving wishes for many
more happier brighter birthdays than this which is rainy without
and busy within.

                                                    Ever yours loving, Lu

*Louisa went to Washington, D.C., at the end of 1862 as an Army nurse.
In early January 1863 she contracted typhoid fever and became deathly ill.
Her father traveled by train to Washington and brought her home, where her
mother nursed her for months.*

★Louisa added later, "Prophetic voice."
†Abigail's sixty-first birthday.

January 1, 1863. A bright, severe winter morning. At 6 o'clock
I woke and seeing a bar of light in the East I rose. Going to the
window I found the stars bright and singing Glory Hallelujah, this
day freedom to the slaves is proclaimed by President Lincoln. God
Bless him for doing this thing, tho' he does it as a *war* measure, a
policy rather than as a *right*. Before 1864 he will see that *righteousness*
must save the nation, and justice to the Black Man alone can now
save this people.

To Dorothea Lynde Dix,
superintendent of Army nurses

Concord, February 8, 1863

D[ea]r Madam,

The total absorption of time and mind since our daughter's
return from Geo[rgetown] has alone prevented our giving expression to the gratitude we feel to yourself, Miss Dix, and other ladies
associated in the hospital duties where Louisa was penned. Her
situation was a most critical one when she left you and she arrived
none too soon to be saved from a most violent typhoid fever. She
has had it, but not as badly as we feared. And I trust with the returning consciousness of house, its comforts, and the presence of dear
friends, she will soon recover. She has great recuperative powers
and a normal condition of health that has often stood the test of
sudden attacks and left her but superficially damaged. Believe us
most gratified and obliged for the tender care you extended to her.
May you be blessed in your mission is the wish and prayers of us all.

Most respectfully,

Abby May Alcott

By spring Louisa felt well enough to write. She began working on short sto-
ries, some based on her war experiences, and adapted her letters home from the

army hospital for publication, first in serial form and then as a book, Hospital Sketches, *which came out that summer and was well received.*

Journal entries

March 28, 1863. Mr. Alcott returns from Boston this weekend bringing the news that Anna is the happy mother of a boy . . . *my first grandchild.* . . .

May 22nd. Anna and her baby arrive, the first visit of my first grandchild to my home. . . . Louisa and Abby go with Una and Julian [Hawthorne] to see the review of the Colored Regiment in Readville, Mr. Emerson and Edith also, they had a nice time. . . . On Tuesday Anna leaves with baby, we miss the darling, his little coo and smile is a perfect sunbeam, how can I live without them, 8 weeks old the 23rd, so bright gentle and tender. . . . I have never had a living son. I cannot complain when I have had the comfort of four good daughters, none better on the earth.

May 1863. Louisa preparing and printing her *Hospital Sketches,* in the *Commonwealth*; they are well received.★

June 14, 1863. This success [of Louisa's] will embolden her, I hope, to greater effort. Sure am I [that] success awaits some special achievement. Her thoughts and purposes have been maturing for some deeper surprise than we have yet had, and I predict that she does not fail to establish a stable position among authorships. It may take years, but she will have no mean ranks assigned her now. She is in the vestibule of the Temple, but the high Altar is not far off. . . .

July 1863. Her story "Debby's Debut" appears in the Atlantic Monthly for Aug[us]t. She is gaining steadily for the confidence.

★Here she copied a June 10, 1863, letter from Henry James Sr. to Louisa, complimenting her "charming pictures of hospital service."

I know of no one who has more modestly sought it [success], and more distrustingly acknowledges it.

August 25, 1863. [Louisa's] life has been most varied and disappointing, but clouds and doubt seem cleared, fairly routed from her horizon by her talents, and perseverance. If her health continues she will earn an honorable independence for herself and much comfort for us, filling our last days with a pride and joy which only parents can feel who have waited long to see their children blest with means to live, and fair chances in the great arena of life. . . .

In the fall of 1863, a publisher accepted Louisa's novel Moods, *which she dedicated to her mother.*

Journal entry

October 19, 1863. God bless and prosper this offspring of her labour, this work of her toiling brain. . . . I think it [*Moods*] will be favorably accepted by the public. She needs this encouragement to promote self appreciation. Her powers are greater than she knows. It must come to her in the palpable form of money and praise to convince her of the bright standard of her power and capabilities.

Old Age

A favorite quotation, copied into Abigail's journal

Could you have the life of any man really portrayed to you, sun-drawn as it were, its hopes, its fears, its revolutions of opinion in each day, its most anxious wishes attained, and then, perhaps, crystallizing into its blackest regrets, such a work would go far to contain all histories, and be the greatest lesson of love, humility and tolerance, that men had ever read? Now fiction does attempt something like the above. . . . The writer of fiction follows his characters into the recesses of their hearts. There are no closed doors for him. . . . [I]t is not to be wondered at that the majority of readers should look upon history as a task, but tales of fiction as a delight.

—Sir Arthur Helps, *Friends in Council:*
A Series of Readings and Discourse Thereon,
1848

Journal entries

Jan 14, 1865. [My] Journal is a very irregular affair. Louisa is reading over my Journals, from 1842, with many intermissions. Still they are land marks by which to note the passage of time. Our lives have all been in the same boat and that gives a relative value to the "Log-Book" tho' not very accurately kept by the pilot. A boat much buffeted about by adverse winds and rough tides, but as we near the port we seem to be having serene skies, gentler gales, firmer hold on the helm and I sing a jolly song with the old British sailor, "Luff boys! Luff!! Don't make wry faces. She rights, she rights. They're safe off shore."

Louisa went to Europe in the summer of 1865 as the paid companion of a young woman. She traveled in Switzerland, Germany, France, and England, and returned to Concord in July 1866 to continue supporting her family. Two years later, in 1868, she would publish her first juvenile novel, Little Women, *which became a bestseller. Abigail would never again have to worry about money.*

July 20, 1866. [Louisa] has resumed her writing for the papers. Her success is without a doubt.★

September 15, 1867. My cousin S.E. Sewall with his wife and daughter Louisa spent Sunday with us, quite a memorable occasion for me. He has been a kind, care-taking friend through my married life, being one of the few friends who understands the peculiarities of our situation, and rightly appreciates the embarrassments and hindrances to our success in life. But this life has not been a failure. Oh no, I look in vain for a longer better womanhood than my daughters have established, or a finer life than my husband leads.

January 1, 1868. Fine quiet snowstorm, like a white shroud on the past, 67 years of my life are laid aside. Its record is not all I could have wished. But it has not been a life carelessly or thoughtlessly spent. My youth was sickly and much indulged in consequence. My girlhood nervous and willful. My womanhood has compensated by its sacrifices, labors and love for all the indiscretions, prejudices, and much uncharitableness. "She loved and was forgiven" is often in my mind, and soothes a contrite soul. . . .

★Someone, probably Abigail, later added, "Prophetic."

January 13. Louisa busying herself while here making me a warm winter dress, of "Linsey Woolsey," a kind of fabric very common when I was young, cotton and wool. . . .

Monday, January 15. All alone! Alone! Alone! Alone! Cutting out work for Katy and myself.★ I love all family employments but cooking. I think I should live on rice and apples, if I lived alone, no! I should have a cordial cup of tea once a day.

Saturday January 18, 1868 . . . John and Freddie are expected.† Make my boys each a picture book. I think I could work for children all the time, and feel amply compensated in their pleasure, tacitly expressed by a smile.

Louisa hears Fanny Kemble, and meets her afterwards. . . .‡

March 1, 1868. Bright and cold. Reading Johnson, my brother having sent me the 6 vols. which belonged to my father, a book I read when I was 10 years of age, and I look it over with pleasurable sensations and sad reminiscence, for the places are no more in which I spent an innocent happy childhood.

. . . 8th Oct.§ My husband presents me with his book "Tablets," Louisa with her book "Little Women," Anna new fur shoes, May with handkerchiefs, Freddy with cuffs. . . .¶

Oct 22nd Came to Maplewood [north of Boston] with Anna and the boys, a neat pretty house, good neighborhood [and] lovely scenery. Am enjoying the warmth and comfort of a neat house. John is a good provider, and thinks of all the little improvements for facilitating good housekeeping.

★She was teaching her niece Katy, a daughter of her late brother Charles, to sew, as she had taught her daughters.

†Abigail's grandsons were now four and two years old, respectively.

‡Fanny Kemble, the famous British actress, was married to an American.

§Abigail's sixty-eighth birthday.

¶Here she pasted a newspaper advertisement for the children's magazine *Merry's Museum*, edited by Louisa.

I wish I might consistently . . . pass my winter and the last few years now left me in this sweet home of peace and comfort [with Anna, John, and their sons]. Perhaps some arrangement can be made for me by which May and Mr. Alcott can be cared for and leave me more free.

My health seems failing, tho' I find with care I keep comfortable. I feel as if 40 years of care, labor, anxiety, and poverty cheerfully born [sic] deserve rest and competence.

November 16, 1868. Leave home from Maplewood last Sat[urday] to make some arrangements for the winter. Quite unsettled in my mind whether I had better risk a cold winter here [at Orchard House], or accept Anna's hospitalities in her snug house at Maplewood. It will be decided for me I think before many days. It is only since my impaired health and defective sight that I even considered myself. My husband's comfort and the best interests of my family have always had my first consideration.

August 30, 1869. Louisa receives from her publisher Roberts & Co. $1000 for her "Little Women" second payment. She places it in the hands of Samuel E. Sewall to be invested with the $200 given him in June, making the sum of twelve hundred dollars since August 30th.

October 20, 1868 . . . Louisa's health being feeble she and May take rooms at 43 Pinckney St[reet in Boston] at Mrs. Singleton's. . . .

Dec[ember] 19, 1869. My brother [Samuel Joseph] comes this week to see me.

20th. S.J. [Samuel Joseph] and Louisa passed the day and night with us [in Concord]. Anna [was] full of hospitality and kindness. Uncle parted saying "dear creatures, lovely family, goodbye darlings." . . .

29th. Niles pays Louisa 2,500 dollars on 6 months sale of "Little Women."★ The following notice appears in the Transcript of the

---

★Thomas Niles was the publisher of *Little Women*, at Roberts Bros.

29th Dec. 1869: Her [Louisa's] connection with this firm of Roberts Brothers has been most appreciable and profitable. Her book "Little Women" has reached the 36 thousandth edition, a remarkable success for a book of so little pretension, and so free from sensational plot.

Feb 22, 1870. Pass most of the day with Louisa and May at their rooms in Pinckney St., Boston. They are preparing for their voyage to Sorrento, South of Italy. Louisa's [hoarse] voice [is] better, May finishing up with her classes.

23rd. My Uncle May dies, 93 years of age.★ Brother S[amuel] J[oseph] officiates at the funeral, having been telegraphed for at Washington on the 24th.

In March 1870 Louisa and May left for a grand tour of Europe with a friend, Alice Barrett. While they were gone, on November 26, 1870, Anna's thirty-nine-year-old husband, John Pratt, died after a short illness. Louisa, who was in Rome, immediately began writing Little Men *so "that John's death may not leave A[nna] and the dear little boys in want." In June, aware that her family could not survive long without its breadwinner, she returned to America.*

Journal entries

June 11, 1871. Our home is full of joy sunshine and roses. Louisa here, comfortable health, great success in her book "Little Men." 36 thousand copies already sold within 2 weeks of its announcement. . . .

June 21, 1871. My brother very sick at Syracuse.

Abigail's brother Samuel Joseph, age seventy-three, died on July 1, 1871, leaving her the only surviving member of her first family.

★Uncle Samuel May was her father's younger brother.

April 20, 1872. I arrange my books, papers, now number and index my Diaries—not of much literary merit, but as history of our lives as a family, struggling with adverse circumstances, each journal as I look it over seems to carry me into scenes of intense interest, either of activity, of suffering, of hopefulness, of doubt. On the whole they give evidence of faithful effort to do and be the best for my own soul's welfare, and the advancement of the best purposes of my family. . . . [Louisa has] by the power of her pen secured not only an universal reputation for good writing, but secured a maintenance for herself and family, having well invested several thousands before the age of 40. What more could I have hoped for? One thing, good health. Here may prove the bitter drop in this cup overflowing with success. She may rally. She has a fine constitution. . . .

Last Sabbath of 1872. I fear little, I hope much, for malice finds no place as an element in the composition of my character. I am impulsive but not *vindictive*. I love long, love much and hope to be forgiven. My education was defective. My married life has been filled with trials. I was not prepared for [it], and hardships I resisted rather than accepted or mitigated. I writhed under the injustice of society, and mourned my incompetency to *live above it*.

December 31, 1872. Another year is closing upon my life. The new year finds us as a family somewhat separated. Mr. Alcott at the west, Louisa in Boston, but having Anna and her children with us. . . . If Louisa's health and capabilities for writing do not get exhausted, she has a fortune before her in her own gift. May has talent and industry to supply all her rational needs. Anna and her boys have got a good start in the world. Everything seems tending to independence.

To Louisa, inside the cover
of Abigail's journal for 1874

Jan[uar]y 1st, 1874

To my Louisa! Beloved daughter,

I place at thy disposal of your judgment this, and all other of my Diaries; to keep for reference, or to destroy for safety, my hopes, fears, aspirations, have been uttered fearlessly, believing this utterance, or prayer or complaint should be known only to that power which can bestow, protect, or relieve.

May you survive me, to consummate to perfection, the march of life you have so nobly begun, so successfully pursued, so generously shared with those whose exertions have been thus far, pursued with less success or reward.

May you have good health as you have the good heart to live and love, *Long! Long!*

Marmee

Journal entries

January 25, 1875. I often feel happier, after putting down some of my *own* experiences [in my journal], than I do in reading much. Novels, even if they are good, pass out of my memory very rapidly. I enjoy it as I should a scene at the theatre; but am not essentially benefitted by the incidents or morals. What more desirable at this period of my life, than to find sources of daily peace and joy from within; that I think is true life. . . .

If [women] can emancipate the slave, . . . they must work out their own emancipation.

April 19, 1875. At the age of 75 years I begin to feel through them (women) the injustice of "Taxation, without representation." This generation, better cultured [and] educated up to the knowledge of their Rights . . . must claim and secure them. First prove they know them, then live and defy the government that withholds them.

If [women] can emancipate the slave, and educate the boys and girls of this generation, they must work out their own emancipation. They [women] must help make the Laws, Be educated as Jurists, Drs. Divines, Artists, Bankers. It will occupy and give dignity to their minds and lives, rear for the nation beautiful girls and powerful boys, [and] learn to control their own homes.

As she had done more than twenty years before, Abigail spearheaded a petition for women's suffrage and equal rights. This petition, too, was discarded by the men of the Massachusetts legislature as if it were "a spent cigar."

May 1, 1875. Concord seems wonderfully indifferent to the whole subject [of women's suffrage].

October 30, 1875. [I am] Reading for the 20th time *Moods*. I look upon this early effort of Louisa's at novel writing [as] quite remarkable. There are in this [book] indications of intellectual power hardly discoverable in any of her subsequent lesser writings.* Her descriptions of scenes, motives, are admirable. I am charmed with it as a piece of fine writing.

Note to Louisa

February 1876. I have been reading over my letters to my dear Brother Samuel J. though thirty years of my married life, and am surprised at the history of my life therein continued. My utterances about politics and the men in power at that period were as prophetic as Charles Sumner's. And I am relieved to find that I was not as

---

*Abigail seems to compare *Moods* favorably to Louisa's later juvenile literature.

busy about my own cupboard and dishpans as I supposed, for in my greatest destitution, I could stop to throw my stone of indignation at Congress, or sniff at the cold charities extended to the needs of others.

In the early fall of 1876, Louisa, forty-three, gave her seventy-five-year-old mother an empty diary, which would be her last. Louisa now lived with her parents, older sister, and two nephews, Fred and John, at Orchard House. Her younger sister, May, thirty-six, had just sailed for Europe to pursue her drawing and painting.

Abigail's last diary

September 19, 1876, [given to] Abby May Alcott from "Louisa."

Sept 20. I dedicate this journal to "May" and this first page to the joyful record of her arrival at Queenstown.

September 30. Let me gratefully acknowledge the relief I enjoy on the receipt of this good news. . . . [I feel] apprehension lest the wild winds and more tempestuous waves may deprive me of these precious girls when on these goings and comings from foreign lands. My nerves are terribly morbid, but reason comes to my aid, and religion adjusts the balance of my faith. . . . I hope to pass the next year in some profitable employment as the days occur and then by reading clever books, seeming cheerful, joyous, doing some light housework as my infirmities will permit of. . . .

October 1. Received our 1st letter from May. . . . She says, "my dear Marmee, While the Capt. promises to keep the boast steady, I scribble a line to assure you of my safe arrival; although the telegraph has long since reached you through the 'Transcript.' The first two days, I was pretty miserable, wondering how I could ever have left my own sweet home, lying in the close, horrid smelling berth, no air, or light; and most of all no Marmee to pet me. The Capt.

came often to see me, and Dr. Hosmer kindly sent me delicious pears to cool my parched mouth. By Wednesday I was feeling better and went on deck, escorted by the Capt. who has been very attentive. Everybody received me with marked attention, so you see the horrors of sea life are greatly mitigated by meeting much kindness from comparative strangers. . . . The Capt. offers to take any parcel back to America next week for me, so I shall try to get the hose for you and Louy. The Scotch Lady our passenger in the *China* spoke charmingly of Louisa as a writer, and begged to see her picture if I had one which of course I had. She talked much of her, and her works, *Little Women* ever so much. . . . Louisa's fame reaches over the sea and makes a welcome for us every where. I hope to get off a long letter for you by next week, kisses all round, no forgetting my Rosa.* I dream of the star on her forehead."

I have thus transcribed the part of dear May's letter because it seems always more precious than anything which may come after as it is the assurance from her hand that she is there bodily safe. Let me be thankful to God for this and all other mercies. I seem to be living beyond the length of days allotted to most, and yet my blessings are without number still.

8th October. [My] 76 birthday. Glorious bright day, the air is full of color, my mercies thicken fast; good news from dear May, Johnny rapidly recovering, Freddy well, Anna and Louisa still saved from infection of typhoid, although they have been over the patient little fellow for 8 days. But my blessings are renewed every day and I am here to receive and record the same.

> *Thus far the Lord has led me on,*
> *Thus far his power prolongs my days!*
> *And every evening shall make known*
> *Some fresh memorial of his Grace!*

———

*Rosa was May's horse.

This afternoon the remains of our friend Miss "Sophia Thoreau" are brought here (her former home) for internment. . . . Henry her brother died in 1864, the mother in '72. Their Cemetery Lot is near ours, which contains only the dear dust of my Lizzie, and close by the bones of our Beloved John Pratt.

My birthday was celebrated tenderly by gifts, fruit, flowers, frills. From Johnny "note-paper" of various tints, very handsome.

She pasted here notes from her grandsons:

To Grandma from Johnny

> *Hid in this box*
> *Pretty paper doth dwell;*
> *A loving wish*
> *And a very good smell.*

To Grandma from Freddy

> *A tidy tie*
> *For grandma's neck,*
> *When the new ruffs*
> *Her bosom deck.*

December 31, 1876. The last day of this Centennial year commemorated by the great world's "Exposition" at Philadelphia. Also the prolonged contest for the Presidential vote owing to false counts at the South, and questionable returns made by the clerks as well as Electors. The Senate will finally have to decide on one of the candidates, or choose a new one. Among so many factions, any choice now will probably lead to great dissatisfaction among the Republicans and Democrats. As a family we have had a comfortable year.

Louisa has published "Silver Pitchers" and "Rose in Bloom" this year, besides several stories; her popularity increases. May's absence is much mitigated by her pleasant letters, and pictures she sends me, and wholly compensated for in the fact of her advantages of Society and Art Culture she enjoys in Paris. I close the brief record of the year 1876 with great gratitude for the comforts I enjoy.

    January 1st, 1877, Concord Mass. . . . Brilliant, beautiful day. The year comes in festively; its gorgeous drapery of clouds of many colors. Not cold. I sew a little for Louisa. Freddy played the piano last night, the last tune, "America," ushers in the New Year with his favorite waltz (*Star*). We take a sleigh-ride, call at Mrs. Pratt's.*
I still find much difficulty in getting into a carriage. My knee is so stiff the whole limb is unmanageable under those conditions. Otherwise I am very well, and enjoy life in a tranquil partial serenity I hardly thought I could reach after such a disturbed condition of the nervous system.† I was fearful that my brain would never fall into any kind of harmonious activity and that paralysis would touch all its centres. . . .

Abigail pasted here a newspaper clipping, "Ruskin says May Alcott, daughter of the Concord seer, now studying art in London, is the only artist worthy to copy Turner. . . ."

    Only gossip. Ruskin never said that.
    January 25. Unexpected pleasure, a letter from May. . . . I try to be satisfied with once a week, but two letters does give me a very refreshing sensation and tones down the blues most astonishingly. She had a fine time at the Healy reception, Miss Peckham accom-

----

*John Pratt's parents still lived in Concord.
†In the summer of 1873 Abigail had suffered "dropsy of the brain," perhaps due to a stroke, from which she recovered after a few months.

panied her. She danced first with Mr. Healy, served through the evening with ice cream and *hot* punch. The whole affair very elegant and effective; went home before 12 o'clock, moderate for Paris.

M. Muller praised [her painting of] the Prince "Timbuktu." . . .

February 1st, 1877. Dr. Dudley of Milwaukee passes the night here, goes to Emerson's for a talk in the evening; Sanborn takes tea with him and they have high talk. The weather was very fine all the time. He talked about Louisa. I showed him the pretty hymn she wrote when 13 years of age in her "little diary," "The Kingdom of God is within you."

Mr. Charles offered to compile a Sunday School chapbook and wrote to Louisa for a contribution of juvenile poetry; she remembered this [hymn], and on reading it over she felt she could do nothing so good now. In her return note to Mr. C she offered, so characteristic, "I send you a little piece which I found in an old journal of my childhood; coming as it does from a child's heart, where conscious of its weaknesses and its wants, it may touch the heart of other children in like mood. Louisa M. Alcott."

22nd February. Louisa returns after an absence of 6 weeks in Boston. We are glad to get her back amongst us in this dreary weather, it creates a new atmosphere in the house, and we all feel more protected when she is about us. She seems quite well and happy. Her success in writing is quite remarkable, and her reputation is made for all future time, as the best writer for young people since Miss Edgeworth and Mrs. Barbauld.* She infuses her morals so skillfully and her ethical machinery is so gracefully concealed by the clinging drapery of love, or the thick foliage of events, that her characters blossom out upon you with ever new grace and beauty as well as truthful to the Life.

----

*Maria Edgeworth, a prominent Anglo-Irish writer, died in 1849. The British author and abolitionist, Anna Laetitia Barbauld, died in 1825.

March 1st, 1877. Louisa takes tea with the Sanborns to confer about the Thoreau house.★

March 2 . . . L[ouisa] goes to Boston.

March 5th. Letter from May. I read with intense interest "Daniel Deronda." It was tedious as a serial but the plot is worked up with the finest intellectual machinery, the author's subtle wit and moral perception, is quite remarkable.

"Hayes and Wheeler," after a long conflict with the Democrats, [were] elected President and Vice President of the United States. The local government of the South are in fearful anarchy, and the financial affairs of the Country in a general state of depression. A new impulse will be given it is to be hoped, to trade, manufacturers and internal improvements under this more honest and prudential government. The last war created fearful factions throughout the country. . . .

March 14. Almost 20 years since we returned to Concord, and here we were called to part with our dear Lizzy. Her dear remains seem to sanctify the place, and here I wish to be laid.

Although I often say it is [of] little consequence where we are finally laid in the flesh, for all dust and earth must receive our corruptible part, yet I must own a preference to the final resting place. To rest amongst our kindred is a desirable thing to look forward to, even if we are insensible to the fact. After that the birds of the air, the dews from heaven, the stars above us, even the snows of winter, are beautiful to contemplate as our companions in their seasons. The daisies will not forget to smile above me, and the sweet clouds of heaven moisten their throats with tender rain. Who can fear death and its consequences if they have repented their sins, hope to be forgiven, and trust all to that power which created, sustained us here and provides such beauty in the natural world to the end.

★Louisa was negotiating to purchase the former Thoreau house on Main Street in Concord for her sister Anna and Anna's two sons.

16th. Anna's [forty-sixth] birthday. We celebrate it, all she is able
to bear, being feeble, with an obstinate cough and cold. A nice letter from May at noon was a pleasant surprise on the occasion. Miss
Reed had brought her a Roman Lamp, like this sketch.* In almost
all her letters May has given me some little sketch of the pretty
things that are collecting about her in Paris. I save them in this way
because I consider this her book, or record of the doings of her
Paris excursion. I think she has realized what a sacrifice to me it has
been to have her gone so far, and has conscientiously tried to gratify
me and her sisters by these frequent and interesting accounts of
her progress in Art, the acquaintances she forms, her criticism of
famous pictures, her hopes of the future, and regrets that these fine
opportunities have come so late in her life.

April 21st. Memorable news from Paris. May's picture admitted
to the great "Art Exhibition" of the season. . . .

May 12, 1877 . . . Great day for the Alcotts. Picture [of May]
arrived from Paris, the hot-bed of High Art, forwarded by Mr. Geo.
Lombard from Liverpool. Miss Peckham has caught May's air and
pose . . . of ten years ago when her eyes were bright, and her heart
was light, and she thought of love and glory. . . . Life itself is short
and swift, music is loud and strong, more sound than harmony.
The picture is "May" and nobody else, but the hat is Madame Milli-
ner's "Salon Chapeau." May's own pretty hair, with her blue velvet
snood, would have suited my taste better, but Paris is all crimson
and gilt, nude or dressed for exhibition.

July 14th. Letters from May. Anna preparing for her new house,
the Thoreau house. Will begin moving on Monday. Another change
in our domestic arrangements. I am persuaded our health will be
better for the change, and it will be better for the boys, nearer their
companions, and the social requirements will be of advantage to
them.

---

*Abigail inserted a pen-and-ink drawing by May of a lamp.

July 15th. My health is good but I am at times feeble, generally weaker. We have two good [servant] women now to do our work; this I hope will prove a relief to Louisa whose cares are too many; and her various responsibilities are unfavorable to her nervous system.

28th . . . [May's] return is still in the far distant of time, but if we are all well, and get these fine letters from week to week, why should we not be content. Life is much the thing we make it, by cheerful endurance of its evils and acceptance of joys, or the anxious forebodings of discontent and ennui.

August 11, 1877. A letter from May. ... . The artist friend, Miss Cassatt, will be her companion for the present; she thinks of going to "Versailles," and "Trianon," on a pleasant excursion, and to the "Theatre Francois"; these little trips will do her good, break up the loneliness of her apartment.

Sept[ember] 1st, 1877. The year nearly closed over May's absence. My health has been unusually good. I have missed her at times very much but each day has brought its occupations and I am here to gratefully record the good progress of her Art, and the good health of the family.

We have had a pleasant call from Miss Putnam, the associate of Miss Holley at Hattiesburg, the colored school. She reaffirms what Miss Holley has often stated of the great utility of this school. The poor Whites beg the permission to come and be taught, for even a little culture makes everything so [much] more respectable for the emancipated blacks that the[y] feel the distinction of races much lessened. Miss P has introduced much of the kindergarten plans, and they succeed remarkably with it. Action, industry is new to them. They are soon made to feel the benefits of order and method. They are taught everything from gardening to sewing and reading.

Our last letters from May announces her safe arrival in England; she hopes to pursue 6 months or a year in studying water-colors. She seems in good heart and hope about her plans for the future.

I am quite irregular about my journal, but my health is so uncertain. Dyspepsia and now constantly increasing difficulties of the heart and chest I suppose and infusion of water. I have a nurse as I require so much care through the night.

Oct. 8th.* The day has been most mercifully extended to me and beautifully celebrated even to the coming of May's letter full of pleasant news.

On the next page is a lock of white hair tied with a black string and, in Louisa's handwriting, "Marmee's pen, left in the book when she had written the last lines, on her 77th birthday, Oct. 8th 1877 at the old home." A few pages later, Louisa added pressed flowers and the words, "Flowers sent us. (Marmee's death)"

On Sunday, November 25, 1877, at Anna's house, into which she and Bronson and Louisa had recently moved, Abigail died. Louisa was with her at the end and closed her eyes, as she had promised. Two days later the Alcotts buried Abigail at Concord's Sleepy Hollow Cemetery, beside Lizzie's grave. Louisa soon received a letter from Elizabeth Palmer Peabody, now age seventy-three.

To Louisa from Elizabeth Palmer Peabody

December 1877

My dear Louisa,

It would do as little justice to myself as to the venerated Mother whom you have lost to mortal vision, but with whom I think you must feel *identified* for ever more, did I not express to you my feelings of intense sympathy, before the privileged days of seclusion are passed by.

I lived with your mother in perhaps the most intense period of

---

*Abigail's seventy-seventh birthday.

her suffering experience of life, and feel as if I knew the heights & depths of her great heart as perhaps only you & Anna can do. For a few months we were separated by stress of feeling in most tragic circumstances, and she doubted my friendship, truth & honor, in strict consequence only because of the depth of my loyalty to her!* But God gave me an opportunity to withdraw the veil & I have in her own hand her written expression of her conviction that I was *true to her* & her deepest worth *at that very time*.

I have never known a great[er], more tender, more selfsacrificing human being; & it was all pure moral force & *character* for she owed nothing to the *Imagination*. It was the tragic element in her that she could not *escape* on *that wing* [of imagination] the full painfulness of *experience*. There was no froth on the cup of life for her. It was all the reality down to its very dregs . . . uprightness & downrightness and plain speech, *but an infinitely tenderer heart,* such a heart as needs *the winged horse* which for fresh air takes daily excursions into the Ideal.

"Ah, me!" said Mr. Emerson once, . . . "it is wonderful how painful is Experience! . . . with the Ideal only is the Rose of Joy!" In all the time & especially the many years of the first part of the time I knew her she was too much without the "Rose of Joy."

It was for you, dear Louisa, in these later years, indeed ever since you grew up, to gather these roses for her & crown her old age with them. You *understood* her—the first person perhaps who ever did sufficiently to do justice to her. Let me congratulate you. "Many daughters have done virtuously—but thou excellest them all."

---

*Elizabeth Peabody was alluding to her conflict with Bronson in 1836, when she taught with him at the Temple School and lived in the same Boston boardinghouse. Abigail's reaction then was to defend her husband. However, even after Miss Peabody "separated" from Bronson, resigned from the school, and left the boardinghouse, she and Abigail had "a little talk" that enabled them to continue their friendship.

Gifted by God with your mother's heart and your father's ideality you united them in yourself, . . . I do not think I ever enjoyed anybody's fictions as I have enjoyed *yours*. I have enjoyed it in imaginative sympathy with both your father and your mother, but especially with the *latter* because she did not forecast the "all is well" as your more imaginative father could do. . . .

Express my sympathy to Anna & your Father; Abby [May] is I believe in Europe & I hope in prosperity.

Yours truly, Elizabeth P. Peabody

Louisa eulogized her mother with a poem.

Transfiguration

Mysterious death! who in a single hour
Life's gold can so refine,
And by thy art divine
Change mortal weakness to immortal power!

Bending beneath the weight of eighty years,
Spent with the noble strife
Of a victorious life,
We watched her fading heavenward, through our tears.

But ere the sense of loss our hearts had wrung,
A miracle was wrought;
And swift as happy thought
She lived again,—brave, beautiful, and young.

Age, pain, and sorrow dropped the veils they wore
And showed the tender eyes

Of angels in disguise,
Whose discipline so patiently she bore.

The past years brought their harvest rich and fair;
While memory and love,
Together, fondly wove
A golden garland for the silver hair.

How could we mourn like those who are bereft,
When every pang of grief
found balm for its relief
In counting up the treasures she had left?

Faith that withstood the shocks of toil and time;
Hope that defied despair;
Patience that conquered care;
And loyalty, whose courage was sublime;

The great deep heart that was a home for all
Just, eloquent, and strong
In protest against wrong;
Wide charity, that knew no sin, no fall;

The spartan spirit that made life so grand,
Mating poor daily needs
With high, heroic deeds,
That wrested happiness from Fate's hard hand.

We thought to weep, but sing for joy instead,
Full of the grateful peace
That follows her release;
For nothing but the weary dust lies dead.

Oh, noble woman! never more a queen
Than in the laying down
Of sceptre and of crown
To win a greater kingdom, yet unseen;

Teaching us how to seek the highest goal,
To earn the true success
To live, to love, to bless
And make death proud to take a royal soul.

Recipes and Remedies

Several of Abigail's "Receipts and Simple Remedies" were found in her borrowed house in Walpole, New Hampshire.

Ginger Snaps

Half pound butter
Half pound sugar
Two and one half pounds flour
1 pint molasses
1 teaspoon soda
Caraway seed or ginger

Roll very thin and bake a few minutes.

Bird Nest Pudding

12 smooth sourish apples cored and laid in a buttered dish open end up, fill the holes with mace, sugar, and lemon gratings. Make rich custard and pour over. Bake one hour.

Currant Shrub

Boil currant juice five minutes with crushed sugar (1 pound) to a pint of juice. Stir constantly while cooking. Bottle when cold.

Buttermilk Biscuit

Pint of buttermilk or sour milk to quart of flour. Rub into the flour a piece of butter the size of an egg, teaspoonful of salt, another of cream of tarter [*sic*]. Stir the milk into the flour. Dissolve a teaspoonful of saleratus and add to it. Add flour enough to make a loaf, roll out inch thick.

Among her "Simple Remedies: A Few Things which Everybody Ought to Know" are:

A quart of peas sown in a shallow box, 15 inches wide by 18 long, at any time of year, and cut when about four or five inches high, and boiled like spinach, with a little salt, makes a most delicious dish. The tops of Jerusalem artichokes, cut off about six inches long, and boiled like greens, makes a capital dish, which partakes in some degree, of the flavor of the root. Boiled water cress also makes a wholesome dish. It must not however be overboiled.

Beat Eggs separately else one bad one may spoil a basin full; when the whites only are wanted, the yolks, if not broken, [can] be kept good if covered. Eggs should be added last of pudding ingredients.

The perfume of fresh flowers may be gathered in a very simple manner, and without apparatus. Gather the flowers with as little stalk as possible and place them in a jar, three parts full of olive or almond oil. After twenty-four hours, put them into a coarse cloth, squeeze the oil from them. Repeat according to the strength of perfume desired. The oil, being thus thoroughly perfumed with the volatile principle of the flowers, is to be mixed with an equal quantity of pure rectified spirits, and shaken every day for a fortnight, when it may be poured off, ready for use.

Chronology

1800   Abigail May, the youngest child of Joseph and Dorothy Sewall May, is born in Boston, October 8.

1801   The Mays and their seven children move to a house on Federal Court, Boston, June 9.

1802   Abigail's six-year-old brother, Edward, dies at home after a fall. Her eldest brother, Charles, goes to sea, leaving a single brother, Samuel Joseph, at home with four sisters.

1805   Abigail begins accompanying Samuel Joseph, three years her senior, to dame school.

1811   Abigail begins keeping a diary, January 1.

1813   Samuel Joseph completes his secondary education at a private "man school," Chauncy Hall, and enrolls at Harvard College.

1815   Abigail is tutored at home.

1815   Abigail's oldest sister, Catherine May Windship, dies in Boston, leaving a husband and small son.

1818   At her father's urging, Abigail is "virtually betrothed" to her twenty-nine-year-old first cousin Samuel May Frothingham, of Portland, Maine.

1819   Abigail moves to Duxbury, Massachusetts, to study history and philosophy for a year with Samuel Joseph's friend the Reverend John Allyn and his schoolteacher sister, Abby Allyn.

1819   Abigail's fiancé dies unexpectedly in August. In December Abigail returns to her parents' house only on the condition that her father not expect her to submit to social calls.

1820   Samuel Joseph, twenty-two, graduates from Harvard Divinity School and begins a career as a minister. Abigail aims to teach or to write, two of the few professions open to women.

1821   Abigail's sister Elizabeth dies in Portland, Maine, leaving a husband and two small children. Abigail provides much child care to her late sister's children in the 1820s.

1822   Samuel Joseph moves to Brooklyn, Connecticut, to become the state's first Unitarian minister.

1825   Samuel Joseph May marries Lucretia Flagge Coffin, June.

1825   Abigail's mother dies at home in Boston in October.

1826   Abigail's father marries Mary Ann Cary, a widow twenty-six years his junior, in October.

1826   Abigail moves with her young charges, a niece and a nephew, to live indefinitely in Brooklyn, Connecticut, with her brother and Lucretia, now one of her closest friends.

1827   A. Bronson Alcott, an itinerant peddler and schoolteacher from rural Connecticut, arrives at the May house in Brooklyn for a week's stay to discuss public education with Samuel Joseph on July 27.

1827   Abigail corresponds with Bronson, who teaches elsewhere in Connecticut.

1828   In April Bronson moves to Boston at the urging of her brother, who provides him introductions to noted teachers and ministers.

1828   Abigail, hoping to see Bronson, visits Boston in June, pursues him, and raises the matter of a proposal in August, when they become engaged.

1829   Still residing in Connecticut with her wards, Abigail urges Boston friends to find Bronson, who is deeply in debt, a paid teaching position so that he and she can marry.

1829   Abigail's sister Louisa dies in Boston, leaving a husband and two children. Charles is still away at sea, so Abigail and Samuel Joseph are the only May siblings remaining in New England.

1830   Dorothy Quincy Hancock, John Hancock's widow and Abigail's Aunt Q, dies in February.

1830   Abigail May marries A. Bronson Alcott at King's Chapel, Boston, May 23.

1830   Samuel Joseph introduces Abigail and Bronson to William Lloyd Garrison, October. Abigail and her brother defy their father and peers by becoming abolitionists.

1830   The Alcotts move in December to a boardinghouse in Germantown, Philadelphia, where Bronson starts a school.

1831   Abigail gives birth to a daughter, Anna Bronson Alcott, on March 16.

1831   Samuel Joseph and the Mays' cousin Samuel E. Sewall assist Garrison in founding the New England Anti-Slavery Society, November.

1832   Abigail gives birth to a second daughter, Louisa May Alcott, in a rented house in Germantown, November 29.

1833   Bronson takes an apartment by himself in Philadelphia to read and write for more than a year, during which he visits his family on weekends.

1833   In December Samuel Joseph cofounds the American Anti-Slavery Society, and Abigail cofounds the Philadelphia Female Anti-Slavery Society.

1834   In August the Alcott family returns to Boston, where they live in a series of boardinghouses while Bronson starts the Temple School.

1835   Abigail delivers a third daughter, Elizabeth Peabody Alcott, in Boston on June 24.

1836   Bronson's teaching assistant Elizabeth Palmer Peabody's *Record of a School* is published. Later, Peabody resigns from the Temple School, dissatisfied with Bronson and concerned about his reputation for eccentricity and blasphemy.

1837   Margaret Fuller, who replaced Peabody as Bronson's teaching assistant, publishes *Conversations on the Gospel,* about

Bronson's teaching at the Temple School, arousing more controversy about Bronson, who closes the school, auctions his belongings to pay debts, and takes in students as boarders.

1837   Samuel Joseph hosts the Grimké sisters at his home in South Scituate, Massachusetts, and becomes the first minister in America to preach for equal rights for women.

1839   Abigail gives birth to a stillborn son in April.

1840   The Alcotts move to rented house in Concord that they cannot afford. Abigail gives birth in Concord to her fourth living daughter, Abigail May Alcott, on July 27.

1841   Colonel Joseph May dies in February. His will entrusts Abigail's portion of his estate to Samuel Joseph and a male cousin, preventing Bronson from claiming it. Bronson's debtors sue the estate, sending it into probate for three years.

1842   Bronson spends five months traveling in England while Abigail lives with their four daughters, Bronson's brother Junius, and her brother Charles in Concord from May to October.

1842   Bronson returns from England in October with William Lane, Henry Wright, and Lane's ten-year-old son, Henry, who move into the Alcotts' Concord cottage. Wright soon departs.

1843   The Alcotts and William and Henry Lane move in June to Fruitlands in Harvard, Massachusetts, to create a utopian community conceived by Bronson and Lane.

1843   Abigail gives Louisa her first journal and encourages her to write, August.

1843   Bronson threatens to leave his family and considers suicide. Abigail and Bronson discuss separating; in December she decides to leave Fruitlands with the children to live in three rented rooms at a nearby farmhouse.

1844   Bronson follows Abigail and their children to the rented rooms on January 16.

1844 Abigail's portion of her inheritance is finally released from probate and made accessible to her trustees.

1845 Abigail instructs her trustees to use her inheritance to purchase a house in Concord, which they name Hillside.

1845 In April the Alcotts move into Hillside, where they will reside for three years, longer than any previous home.

1848 Unable any longer to tolerate poverty, Abigail travels to Waterford, Maine, to work as the matron of a water-cure spa. She works from May to July but, displeased with the spa's management, she resigns her post and returns to Concord.

1848 In November Abigail and her daughters move to Boston, where she is employed as a "sister of charity," feeding, housing, and aiding the poor of Ward 11, now the South End.

1849 Louisa completes her first novel, *The Inheritance*, which was not published in her lifetime. Anna and Louisa work as maids, teachers, and companions to help Abigail feed and house the family.

1850 Bronson, age fifty, begins a flirtatious correspondence with Ednah Littlehale, age twenty-four.

1851 Abigail sells Hillside and is able to rent a house for the family on Boston's Beacon Hill.

1853 Anna travels to Syracuse, New York, to live for several years with her uncle Samuel Joseph's family and teach at an asylum run by her uncle's friend.

1853 Abigail and others petition the Massachusetts legislature for female suffrage. The petition is ignored. Bronson begins the first of many western tours in which he spends three to six months each winter traveling across America giving "conversations."

1854 Louisa's first published book, *Flower Fables,* appears in December.

1855 Abigail and her daughters move to Walpole, New Hampshire, where her brother-in-law has offered her a house and garden rent-free.

1855 Elizabeth and Abby May develop scarlet fever, from which the younger sister soon recovers.

1856 Abigail nurses Elizabeth, consults doctors in Boston.

1858 Elizabeth Sewall Alcott dies in a rented house in Concord, March 14.

1858 The Alcotts purchase and in July move into Orchard House, Concord.

1860 Anna Alcott marries John Pratt at Orchard House on May 23.

1861 Louisa sells short stories and thrillers to serial magazines.

1862 In December Louisa becomes an army nurse and travels to Washington, D.C., to work at an army hospital.

1863 After three weeks as a nurse, Louisa contracts typhoid fever and is sent home. Abigail nurses Louisa from January to March. For the rest of her life Louisa will suffer from a debilitating illness, now suspected to be an autoimmune disorder. In August she publishes a book based on letters she sent to her family from the army hospital, entitled *Hospital Sketches*.

1864 Louisa continues to earn money by writing for "penny-dreadful" magazines.

1865 Louisa travels to Europe for a year, initially as the paid companion of a young invalid woman.

1866 Louisa returns to Concord to resume supporting her family.

1868 Louisa's first juvenile novel, *Little Women,* is published in October and becomes a bestseller, ending forever her family's financial insecurity.

1868 Bronson, age sixty-eight, begins a flirtatious correspondence with Ellen Chandler, age twenty-five.

1869 Louisa publishes the second half of the book now known as *Little Women* in April.

1870 Louisa, her sister May, and a friend travel through Europe for a year.

1871 Louisa publishes another *Little Women* sequel, *Little Men,* dedicated to her two young nephews, Freddy and Johnny Pratt, whose father died in November 1870.

1871 Abigail's only remaining sibling, Samuel Joseph, dies at home in Syracuse on July 1.

1875 On the anniversary of the start of the American Revolution, Abigail again petitions the Massachusetts legislature for female suffrage; again the petition is ignored.

1877 May Alcott travels to Europe to study and teach art in London and Paris.

1877 Abigail moves into her daughter Anna's house on Main Street in Concord, where she dies, with Louisa at her side, on November 24. She is buried at Sleepy Hollow Cemetery beside her daughter Elizabeth.

1878 May Alcott is engaged to Ernst Nieriker, a Swiss businessman eighteen years her junior, in London. Less than two months later, on March 22 they marry in London, with none of her family present.

1878 Bronson and Louisa read over and edit Abigail's voluminous journals.

1879 May Alcott delivers a daughter, Louisa May Nieriker, in Paris on November 8. On December 29, May Alcott dies of childbirth fever.

1880 Ten-month-old Louisa May Nieriker arrives in Boston in October to be raised by her aunt Louisa May Alcott; Bronson soon departs on his final western tour.

1882 Bronson suffers an incapacitating stroke.

1884 Louisa sells Orchard House; she and Anna move with their father and three children to a rented house on Beacon Hill.

1885 Louisa purchases a large Beacon Hill townhouse for her family on Louisburg Square, where she employs a cadre of nurses and servants.

1886 Louisa completes her last juvenile novel, *Jo's Boys.* Frail and unable to continue writing, she moves to a nursing home run by Dr. Rhoda Ashley in Roxbury.

1887   Louisa adopts her nephew John so he can renew her copyrights after her death.

1888   Bronson dies at Louisa's Beacon Hill house on March 4. Two days later, at age fifty-five, Louisa suffers a stroke and dies at the nursing home, March 6.

1888   Anna and her son John accompany eight-year-old Louisa May Nieriker to Switzerland, where she returns to the custody of her father.

1895   Anna dies, survived by her two sons and her niece.

1910   Frederick Alcott Pratt dies.

1912   Orchard House opens to the public as a museum.

1923   John Sewall Pratt Alcott dies.

1971   Louisa May Nieriker dies.

Acknowledgments and Sources

My husband, David, suggested the idea for this collection, which could not have been completed without the insight and encouragement of Lane Zachary, Millicent Bennett, and Chloe Perkins. Rose LaPlante spent so many hours transcribing manuscripts in the Alcott collection at Harvard University that she became adept at reading Abigail May Alcott's penmanship. Lisa Stepanski, the author of *The Home Schooling of Louisa May Alcott,* and Lis Adams, the director of education at the Alcott museum, Orchard House, transcribed original documents and directed me to important materials I might have overlooked. I am grateful also to Cynthia Barton, the author of *Transcendental Wife*, for her encouragement and assistance, and to Megan Marshall and Catherine Rivard for their expert advice.

Harvard University and Orchard House (The Louisa May Alcott Memorial Association) generously permitted me to publish material from the Alcott and May family papers. Many of the writings in this volume are in the Alcott collection at the Houghton Library of Harvard University. Heather Cole, Assistant Curator of Modern Books & Manuscripts at Houghton Library, graciously arranged for permissions. Librarians who assisted me at Houghton—not least in deciphering Abigail's handwriting—include Peter Accardo, James Capobianco, Susan Halpert, Mary Haegert, Micah Hoggatt, Emilie Hardman, Rachel Howarth, Tom Lingner, Leslie Morris, Emily Walhout, and Joseph Zajak. I cannot imagine a more pleasant environment in which to read and transcribe manuscripts than Houghton.

The staff of Orchard House opened their arms to me in the course of researching this volume. I am indebted to not only Lis Adams but also Jan Turnquist and Maria Powers for their advice and support. Several of Abigail's original recipes and remedies, found in the attic of the house that Abigail occupied in Walpole, New Hampshire, in the 1850s, and transcribed for Orchard House by Nancy L. Kohl, appear here by permission of the Louisa May Alcott Memorial Association.

Two newly discovered letters appear by permission of William "Whizzer" Wheeler, of Waterford, Maine, in whose possession they reside. Abigail wrote and sent them in 1848 to her friend Ann Sargent Gage, Whizzer's great grandmother.

At the Kroch Library of Cornell University, I wish to thank director and archivist Elaine Engst, Laura Linke, Katherine Reagan, Connie Finnerty, and Brenda Marston, for their assistance in reviewing family papers in the May Anti-Slavery manuscript collection, Division of Rare and Manuscript Collections, Cornell University Library.

Most of Abigail May Alcott's writings appear by permission of Houghton Library, Harvard University, and Louisa May Alcott's Orchard House. The manuscripts for the majority of these writings can be found in the following collections at Harvard's Houghton Library: Alcott family letters (MS Am 1130 and MS Am 1130.1–1130.2); Alcott family papers (MS Am 1130.4); Alcott family additional papers (MS Am 1130.14–1130.16, MS Am 2745, and MS Am 1817.2); Amos Bronson Alcott papers (MS Am 1130.9–1130.12); Louisa May Alcott papers (MS Am 800.23); and Louisa May Alcott additional papers (MS Am 1817, MS Am 2114, and MS Am 1130.13). The original letters to Abigail from her father and her brother Samuel Joseph are also in the collection of Alcott Papers at Houghton Library. The 1801 doctor's bill for her birth is in the collection of May Papers at the Onondaga Historical Association Museum & Research Center in Syracuse, New York. The 1848 letters from Abigail to Ann Sargent Gage are in a private collection in Maine. The December 1877 letter from Elizabeth Palmer Peabody to Louisa May Alcott is reprinted from Bruce Ronda, ed., *Letters of Elizabeth Palmer Peabody* (Middletown, CT: Wesleyan University Press, 1984), pp. 382–382. Louisa's poem "Transfiguration" is reprinted from *A Masque of Poets* (Boston: Roberts Bros., 1878), in which it appeared anonymously.

Alcott and May scholars whose work I relied on in addition to Cynthia Barton and Lisa Stepanski include Madelon Bedell, Ted Dahlstrand, Sarah Elbert, Elizabeth Lennox Keyser, Joel Myerson, Daniel Shealy, Madeleine Stern, and Donald Yacovone. Others who aided in preparing this volume include Sarah Kozma, a curator of the Onondaga Historical Association in Syracuse; Meg Wheeler; Peter Drummey; Edward Furgol; Elly Urquhart; Liza Hirsch; Virginia LaPlante; Clara Dorfman; Charlotte LaPlante; and Philip Dorfman.

At Free Press, in addition to Millicent Bennett and Chloe Perkins, I wish to thank Martha Levin, Dominick Anfuso, Kathryn Higuchi, Tom Pitoniak, Erich Hobbing, Eric Fuentecilla, and Jill Siegel.

Index

The letter *n* after a page number refers to
the "note" (footnote) on that page.

About the Author

Eve LaPlante is a great-niece of Abigail and a cousin of Louisa May Alcott. She is the author of their dual biography, *Marmee & Louisa*, the biographies *Salem Witch Judge* and *American Jezebel*, and *Seized*. She lives with her family in New England and can be contacted at www.EveLaPlante.com.

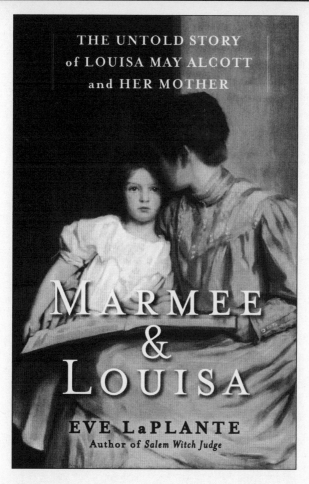